Fat, Pretty, and Soon to Be Old

Fat, Pretty, and Soon to Be Old

A Makeover for Self and Society

KIMBERLY DARK

More Praise for *Fat, Pretty, and Soon to Be Old*

"The latest from Kimberly Dark is exactly what you want her to deliver—it's funny, insightful, heart-breaking, all at once—and it makes you sit back and think about the relationships you have with your own body and life ... Kimberly opens the book calling for radical cultural change, and many of her essays do stir that within you. They also bring forth laughter and tears, anger and joy ... I'm grateful to her for being willing to share herself so honestly with the us through her written and spoken word." —**Dr. Cat Pausé, Fat Studies Scholar, Massey University, New Zealand**

"On stage as, a performer, Kimberly Dark reminds us that the body does not have to be an abstract entity divorced from the story told about it. And now in her book *Fat, Pretty, and Soon to Be Old* she demonstrates how this interplay between narrative and feeling can be achieved with the written word too ... The conversational tone that draws us in camouflages the robust intellectual work that frames the stories. Linking the personal and political with theoretical integrity and without recourse to academic devices for legitimacy, the book serves as an exemplar of a liberatory teaching style. If you're looking for a moving read that is also an important contribution to fat activism this is it." —**Lucy Aphramor, Co-author of *Body Respect: What Conventional Health Books Get Wrong, Leave Out, and Just Plain Fail to Understand About Weight***

"Kimberly Dark's storytelling feels like a joyful visit from a best friend, one who is happy to talk about painful things and—with shared awareness, laughter, and compassion—transmute them into empowerment and enjoyment. Her life stories track family influences, fat liberation, and the joys of embodiment. She's an excellent guide and companion for all of us who navigate personal appearance worries, weight-based hierarchies, and societal oppressions. Start reading now if you hope to feel more yourself and more able to change the world." —**Marilyn Wann, author of *FAT!SO?***

"Kimberly Dark is a staunch believer in the power of storytelling—as a practice for developing compassion, as a tool for self discovery and self love. These intimate essays will resonate deeply for many of us, while tenderly inviting us to consider and create new narratives about bodies, lives, families, and empathy. Dark is a sorceress here, transmogrifying tired stories about people like us—fat folks, queer folks, gender minorities, folks managing disabilities, people harmed and restrained by white supremacy—into spells for solidarity, laughter, and joyful complexity. Dark isn't trying to sell us a reductive idea of self-acceptance as liberation, but she knows, and she shows, that re/writing the stories of our own bodies is critical to our communal struggle toward lasting social change." —**Erin Kate Ryan, author of** *Quantum Girl Theory* **(forthcoming)**

"In *Fat, Pretty and Soon to Be Old*, Kimberly Dark explores the real of her own stories to question the currency of beauty and appearance. What have we actually been sold? What have we bought into about our bodies? Has the exchange ever really been worth the price? In this honest and insightful collection, Kimberly Dark offers us a new story about the body, one I believe we should all buy." —**Sonya Renee Taylor, author of** *The Body Is Not an Apology: The Power of Radical Self Love*

"Nothing is more brilliant and juicy to me than a woman stepping fully into her self—mind, body, and spirit, full throttle, without apology. The day we all step fully into our bodies and voices will be a revolutionary moment. Kimberly Dark has been illuminating the path for a long time. This book is a triumph. This book is a jail break from cultural inscriptions meant to keep us locked up, shut up, and conforming." —**Lidia Yuknavitch, author of** *Book of Joan* **and** *Chronology of Water*

Fat, Pretty, and Soon to Be Old: A Makeover for Self and Society

© 2019 Kimberly Dark
Afterword © 2019 Linda Bacon

ISBN: 978-1-84935-367-0
E-ISBN: 978-1-84935-368-7
Library of Congress Control Number: 2019933798

AK Press	AK Press
370 Ryan Ave. #100	33 Tower St.
Chico, CA 95973	Edinburgh EH6 7BN
USA	Scotland
www.akpress.org	akuk.com
akpress@akpress.org	ak@akedin.demon.co.uk

The above addresses would be delighted to provide you with the latest AK Press distribution catalog, which features books, pamphlets, zines, and stylish apparel published and/or distributed by AK Press. Alternatively, visit our websites for the complete catalog, latest news, and secure ordering.

"Here's Looking at You" appeared in *Hot and Heavy: Fierce Fat Girls on Life, Love, and Fashion*, edited by Virgie Tovar (Oakland: Seal Press: 2012)

"Becoming Travolta" appeared in *Queering Fat Embodiment*, edited by Samantha. Murray, Cat Pause, and Jackie Wykes (Farnham, UK: Ashgate Press, 2014)

"Wanted: Fat Girl" appeared in *Whistling Fire*, October 2011

"Coming Out Fat" appeared in *Fat Sex: New Directions in Theory and Activism*, edited by Helen Hester and Caroline Walters (Farnham, UK: Ashgate Press, 2015)

"My First Lover was not a Lesbian" appeared in *Persistence: All Ways Butch and Femme*, edited by Ivan Coyote and Zena Sharman (Vancouver, CA: Arsenal Pulp Press, 2011)

"Migration Patterns" appeared in *Inside Relationships*, edited by Sandra L. Faulkner (Walnut Creek, CA: Left Coast Press 2013)

Versions of "The Aging Yoga Body," "Shadow on a Tightrope," "Cozy or Uncomfortable: Tight Public Spaces" and "Self-Help, Fitness, and Feminism" have appeared in these blogs: *Decolonizing Yoga*, *Ms Magazine*, and *Feminist Wire*

Cover photo by Substantia Jones
Cover design by John Yates | www.stealworks.com
Printed in the United States

This book is dedicated to all the children, especially girls, who will grow up without fear of being fat, nor fear of aging, able to focus on the beauty of their experiences and pursuits rather than their appearance. May they love fiercely—each person's humanity, body, and integrity. They're already on their way; I know because I am holding them in heart and vision. Let it be so.

CONTENTS

INTRODUCTION

The repossession by women of our bodies will bring far more essential change to human society than the seizing of the means of production by workers.

—Adrienne Rich

This is not just a memoir told in essays. It's a call for radical cultural change.

My mother sold the dream of life mastery—a chance for sovereignty within the restrictive and persistent landscape of patriarchy. I'm talking about the 1960s now. That was a long time ago, or at least that's what you tell yourself.

At first, that dream of mastery was for white women specifically—but then it included men, children, and people of color as well. It included the rich, middle class, and lower-middle class but never the very poor. It could include queer folks as long as they were gender-conforming. It never included gender-non-binary folks.

My mother went to modeling classes when she was still in high school, in 1949. Her family was working class but white, so they were able to take advantage of the new FHA home loans and buy a house. They were set toward economic improvement, and their only daughter was pretty, so it made sense to give her the skills for upward mobility.

After her modeling school graduation was attended by many of her high school friends, she reaped the rewards of being seen as skilled at beauty, capable of charm. During the 1950s, she was a model herself. That was a time when the women who sold products were nameless smiling beauties, not celebrities. She went on to work for—and eventually owned—a John Robert Powers franchise. Powers's eponymous charm schools began in 1923, and business boomed right up to the Internet age. I believe three social developments took place during the late 1980s and early 1990s in the United States to hasten the decline of modeling and charm schools. One was the increasing use of Internet sharing: not relying on just magazine articles, real people shared beauty secrets online. The second related phenomenon was the slight diversification of beauty ideals. It was possible to find affinity groups and positive representation of women of color, redheads with freckles, and very tall women, for instance. Specific lessons on hyper-conformity began to feel retrograde. The third development to hasten the demise of charm schools was the widespread availability of consumer credit and the ability of doctors to advertise to the general public, which began during the Reagan era. All of these changes made beauty a do-it-yourself endeavor and the body a repair project worthy of medical interventions like cosmetic and bariatric surgery, not just dieting and careful packaging.

Here's the main premise of the charm school era in which I grew up and that still influences the world we live in today: if a woman can figure out how to be beautiful and how to have charm, she is more likely to control her own destiny.

This is not incorrect. And it's a sorry substitution for meaningful social change that would actually allow women respect and the ability to steward their own destinies. When I was born, no matter how pretty or charming or trim, no matter how capable of emotional labor or choosing the right bottle of wine for dinner or enunciating proper English, a woman still could not open a credit card account without her husband's permission. Women could still legally be raped by their husbands. Even today, we are not always able to secure birth control as part of our health plans and certainly not always believed when reporting abuse.

Further, appearance still affects quality of life. A lot. We all know this, yet we subvert our knowing by telling stories about love (in intimate relationships), talent (in employment), and tenacity (in all meaningful pursuits). The fact is, people see their partners' appearance or power (or both) as an extension of their own success. (And you know immediately for which of the two dominant genders each is most important.) Employers want their employees' appearance to uphold and extend their brand credibility, and they won't hire those who are easily disdained (e.g., fat people or old people, unless they are absurdly cute and entertaining). Without reasonable accommodations, no amount of tenacity will help a wheelchair user turn a flight of stairs into a ramp. Yet we still discuss personal tenacity and positive thinking as the key ingredients in overcoming public barriers.

While modeling schools showed women (and others) how to conform to beauty standards, we less often discussed what the particular homogenization of those standards meant to consumer America. People of color were taught to act and dress and appear whiter in order to gain access to everyday advantages. Fat people were taught to "reduce" or give the appearance of disappearance, to blend in. Disabled people were taught to develop personality, to emotionally manage others' expectations regarding their abilities. Conformity to the gender binary was paramount. These are the values with which I grew up, and our family business was to teach people how to navigate social expectations successfully.

And, of course, those lessons cost money. "Personal development" courses were marketed by modeling schools as an investment in one's familial and professional success. While these courses were not the first or only expression of consumerist values in personal improvement, they were a strong precursor to the current-day thinking that encourages us to spend money to improve ourselves. Whereas previous (turn-of-the-nineteenth-century) ideas of self-improvement may have encouraged reading more classic literature, doing good deeds in one's community, or learning to play a musical instrument, current thinking assumes that people—women more than men, people of color more than white people, fat people more than slender people—must engage in appropriate appearance management. The undertaking is so important that rather than learning the skills of fashion, design, and hairstyling, for instance, individuals spend huge sums for professional help to be sure they get it right. Indeed, spending money has become tantamount to expanding personal power, even when it paradoxically leads to impoverishment and long-lasting debt.

You may not have discussed the tools of conformity as openly as my family did (and we didn't discuss it using this language), but you grew up with these norms too. These values didn't just go away because we were learning about them on the Internet or discussing physical modifications with our doctors rather than taking classes in a downtown high-rise after work as in the heyday of John Robert Powers.

The basic idea of "self-improvement"—learning how to better play the game—was benevolent, except that it reinforced a hierarchy to keep racial privilege, social class privilege, and all the other privileges in place. Appearance matters. People behave differently toward you if you're white, well-dressed, pretty, young, gender-conforming. This is another way of saying, as bell hooks so often does, that we live in an "imperialist white supremacist capitalist patriarchy." We can all test the idea that appearance and cultural capital matter using reflections on our own lives. Consider how people spoke about each other's appearance following your last large family gathering. *What was she wearing? Did he really put on that much weight? How does she not know how old she looks with that hairstyle?* Consider the process of job interviewing. With rare exceptions, these experiences uphold hegemonic appearance standards, and, if you are recalling an exception, you are aware that it is indeed an exception to the norm. The criteria by which we judge others—even if we have the compassion not to speak our judgment—betray the cultural values over which we believe we have control.

For instance, most people think they're choosing how to look and expressing individuality without considering the built-in desire for maximum social privilege and how that keeps systems of oppression based on privilege intact. Most don't consider the importance of expressing group solidarity—appearing like one's friend group or political party or profession. With an array of options on the Internet, most don't consider the paucity of choices in local shopping chains and how much of what we order online actually conforms with the inventory already available at the local Home Depot or Marshalls.

These factors drive decision-making. Even when the pursuit of privilege becomes invisible, it is easily revealed by trying to imagine an opposite. Author hooks has also commented on how white supremacy influences everyone—even white people—to aspire to whiteness. Think about the increasing number of salons that specialize in giving patrons blond hair and "natural" highlights, often accompanied by straightening or "blowout" services. Now think about how absurd it would seem to walk past the same salon focused on giving patrons of any race artificial dark afros. Yet somehow we remain uncomfortable talking about the descriptor hooks uses persistently: "imperialist, white supremacist capitalist patriarchy." She reports that people often laugh when she says this, like it's hyperbole, a joke for effect. She reminds us that she's just being concise.

No, we'd rather take on the neoliberal beauty project and lament the fact that hierarchy still exists but that at least we're doing our best not to be at the bottom. When I first started giving public presentations in the 1990s on the distribution of wealth and income based on race and gender, I worked with community-based coalitions. Though they were often quite progressive, they still felt that a focus on how people should dress for interviews would be more useful than showing people how the cultural and political deck has been stacked against them.

"Couldn't we videotape people so they could see how their lower-class ways, words, and appearance are defeating them?" I was asked. "Shouldn't we be focused on changing the individuals? People need immediate results." And, "Hey, what if we have a drive for plus-size business wear for women. That'll help." The thing is, these tactics do help some people who are on the edge of appearance acceptability. But they will never help restructure economic opportunities, revise policies, or lead to true inner peace about how one looks. These tactics may pull up a "movable middle," but they will always keep a social hierarchy, with a clear top and bottom, intact.

Look, I get it. So much of what's influencing our lives seems out of our control. We just want to know what we can do to make things better. That's why the neoliberal nonsense about self-improvement enhancing upward mobility (primarily via educational degrees and appearance modification) seems so attractive. Of course, personal improvement goals like degrees, weight loss, and wardrobe improvement overwhelmingly serve to feed the consumerist growth monster of debt and bolster the notion that we are not worthy unless we look and achieve in certain ways. That is, these aims actually rob of us of time, money, and personal sovereignty. The idea that people can assume debt in order to create a better future is the leading personal paradox of our time.

Nowadays, dieting and dressing well are not enough. Doctors (wrongly) say that the body can be safely and surgically slenderized, noses trimmed, breasts enhanced—and all on an affordable payment plan. And if you still feel badly about how you look for any reason, add body positivity to your to-do list because failing to love your body is yet another personal problem to be solved. Self-esteem is sexy; confidence helps you become employable; loving yourself improves health.

In her book, *American Plastic*, Laurie Essig calls the widespread availability of plastic surgery and consumer credit "the perfect storm." She also points out that we are acculturated as consumers to believe that these entail our personal desires rather than cultural conformity. As she explains in the chapter "Learning to Be Plastic," "To keep beauty profitable, our bodies must be colonized as if they were foreign lands. In this way, beauty can create new markets and extract more wealth."

My body has been used to frighten people into doing something about their own, so as not to become like me. I've often been targeted by advertising campaigns and doctors for surgical interventions, which I've not pursued, so you won't read about those experiences in this book. I hope it is clear that we are all influenced by living in a culture that sees these efforts as reasonable self-improvements despite the health and financial risks. The intersections of various forms of appearance privilege, along with the intertwined pursuits of credibility based on social class or educational attainment, are also explored here. Sociologist Pierre Bourdieu extended Marx's idea of capital into the realm of the cultural, and that's the thinking I apply here. Marx distinguished capital from money. Money to buy goods or services is just money. Capital is money that is used to buy things in order to sell them again. Capital creates wealth, which is intertwined with social relationship. Appearance privilege and the hierarchy it creates can be understood in similar terms.

Bourdieu refers to the "symbolic" collection of skills, mannerisms, credentials, accent, posture, et cetera that comprise the tool kit of privilege, of which we are often unconscious. Those tools are rarely used in a quid pro quo arrangement—to purchase a specific commodity. Like Marx's idea of capital, they are used to barter toward greater gain across time and within relationships. We create additional social capital based on where we work, with whom we associate, and how we seem to significant audiences. That is, our agreement on what constitutes beauty matters. Our perpetuation of the means to create and achieve hegemonic beauty matters a great deal.

In many ways, the modeling school era of my youth and of my mother's generation were more honest in their pursuit of that privilege. They knew that privilege was the aim—to be seen as someone with a model's beauty would yield complex personal and professional rewards. The coursework did not just include how to shape the body through hunger, color, shading, and clothing; it included how to enunciate clearly, use refined diction, choose wine at dinner, and steward a scintillating conversation during the meal.

As if our participation in upholding these standards for the sake of corporate profit weren't nefarious enough, we tend to accept that some people just have a certain "way about them," a feel for being slender, youthful, and attractive, while others don't. Our belief in beauty, charm, and charisma adds to its capital. Some women just don't feel good enough about themselves. That's a shame, we might say, but it's up to them to remedy the situation. We don't even see that it is within our collective ability to amend that circumstance for all women. Now that body positivity is the new marketing edict, if a woman doesn't present flawless love and acceptance of herself, she's also to blame for the shame and awkwardness that others witness.

Of course, feeling positive about one's appearance is not just a personal problem, though painful self-image can assail anyone. Bourdieu explained how this reinforces the idea that some people are worthy of receiving social rewards while others are not. Capitalism and all forms of class society shore up and reproduce themselves by dividing people. The obvious divisions have to do with social class, but the history of racism in the United States is another fine example. Our forebears simply invented another appearance-based distinction on which to base distribution of resources. We are still living with the vibrant consequences of deciding that when we look at some people, we are witnessing less humanity, even though the period of their servitude has formally ended. (Note that when I say "we" I am not speaking on behalf of whiteness. I am speaking on behalf of United States culture. Even those who are oppressed internalize a diminished humanity, until we are able to believe and behave otherwise.)

Very few people consciously want this to be so. People want to feel comfortable. The startling paradox here is that love and connection are the most comforting things humans know. Yet most people are daily reinforcing capitalist divisions that keep us alienated from the love we might otherwise feel for one another's bodies and for the beauty of human diversity. This, at its most fundamental—the inability to love and value our own *and* other people's bodies—is what keeps human culture disdainful, violent, and purchasing in order to alleviate our suffering. Consumerism—some might say capitalism itself—feeds itself when it feeds on our desire for connection and personal respect.

We have to cultivate the ability to look at other people's bodies and love them with an expansive agape. We have to care for our own and other people's bodies with compassion and tenderness. The mechanisms that reproduce inequality have become invisible. I believe that through storytelling we can reveal them again.

Body positivity will never be enough. As it's presented in advertising and media, body positivity is not about doing away with beauty conformity. It is merely calling attention to the fact that beauty conformity is important enough that *you* should be allowed into the club. By saying that a slightly wider variety of bodies should be seen as acceptable—maybe not optimal, but acceptable—the importance of beauty conformity is solidified. There is nothing radical about this. As Amanda Mull offered in "Body Positivity Is a Scam,"

> Like most ideas that become anodyne and useless enough for corporate marketing plans, "body positivity" didn't begin that way—it started out radical and fringe, as a tenet of the fat acceptance movement of the 1960s. Back then, body positivity was just one element of an ideology that included public anti-discrimination protests and anti-capitalist advocacy against the diet industry, and it made a specific political point: To have a body that's widely reviled and discriminated against and love it anyway, in the face of constant cultural messaging about your flaws, is subversive.
>
> Now body positivity has shed its radical, practical goals in favor of an advocacy that's entirely aesthetic and a problem that can be wholly solved by those looking to sell you something. The brands previously thought you should feel one way about yourself, and now they have decided that's no longer appropriate for their goals. How you talk about yourself should change, even if nothing has changed that would materially affect how you feel.
>
> The way these companies see it, our self-perception is unrelated to the external forces that determine the circumstances of our existence, which is why they think telling us to do better is enough to absolve them of responsibility.

So when do we get to not only see the bigger picture but hold it long enough to modify it? As the title of this book says, I'm soon to be old. I'm not kidding about that shit. As a woman who is fat, pretty, queer, and aging, among other things, I have a perspective that might help us reach critical mass as we discuss social change. Sure, wear the "body shaper" if you think it's going to help you not be ridiculed on the bus. Put on some makeup if it's going to help you be heard in the job interview. I'm not against the savvy application of social knowledge. But let the application of social knowledge be this: artful manipulation of privilege, not a daily quest for privilege that leaves existing power structures unchecked.

When it comes to those power structures, it matters how we talk and behave, what we wear, and which norms we challenge in small ways, day after day after day. We are creating culture even as it creates us. It matters that we check our own stories, discuss common words and phrases with our friends, and prepare for the moments that will happen again and again throughout our days, months, years, and lives. Before this day is through, someone will discuss dieting again in your presence. Unless you're reading this in bed at 11:00 p.m., I can almost guarantee it.

We have to get ready, think clearly, behave differently, speak openly, and show who we are and what we want the world to be. No more just talking in private or just thinking about how we're not comfortable when someone says, "Fat big-lip bitch" to the black female fast-food worker who's slowly helping the person ahead of you in line. What's happening in that comment? We have to own what we know, prepare to interrupt the culture as it is and become cultural creators.

Before someone can see you, you have to *be* you. I'm going to show you who I am in these pages with the hope of prompting urgency with this practice. I'm going to show you because I respect you. I believe in our ability to make the world a better place before we die. That's what I care about. Not staying pretty. Not losing weight. I care about justice. See how you feel as you read; I hope your own creativity is sparked in the process too.

I.

MAINTAINING APPEARANCES

My small suburban private school was structured to provide two years of preschool and then kindergarten at age five. I was a big child and smart, so partway through my first year of preschool, I was moved into the kindergarten class with Mrs. Shalala and the older kids. I didn't yet know how to write my name, but luckily there was another girl named Kimberly in the class. On the first day we were given pencils and paper, and I sat next to her and did my best to copy what she wrote. I started to get nervous when she stopped after the "m." As the fearsome Mrs. Shalala came around checking our progress, I leaned to my neighbor and asked, "Aren't you going to write the rest?" Our name was a long impressive mess. I was especially unsure how to manage that "y" at the end. It was meant to drop below the solid line on the page, and I didn't want to get it wrong. She beamed at me and said, "That's all you have to put."

No one had ever called me "Kim" before, only "Kimberly," and Mrs. Shalala showed me how to make the big proud-looking capital D with a period to represent my last name, and thus began my formal schooling as Kim D.—a character I had never been in my short life.

The wisdom to move me up was questionable, but I did fine by watching and mimicking and trying to understand how things were done in the upstairs classroom led by the lady with the big white hair. My size made me look like all the other kids, like a five-year-old, though I was still just three. It was considered a good thing to be of conforming appearance; that much was clear to me. The preschool classroom was on the patio-level of our school, with access onto a small playground that was only for us. Mrs. Shalala's room was upstairs, and it was all blue—walls, carpet, tables, and the sky I could see from the windows of our lofty perch. She was sort of mean. I was tempted but fearful to take part in her torment of the other kids. She asked us questions as a group and required a response in unison. We learned through repetition and unspoken expectation mostly. She instructed us to add her name to the end of our responses. She'd say something like, "How are you today, class?" And we'd say in unison, "Very well, thank you, Mrs. Shalala." She'd say, "Class, are you going to have all of the art supplies put away neatly before lunch?" Then she'd look forebodingly at the clock that showed the two lines not quite straight up and we'd call back, "Yes, Mrs. Shalala."

The resistance the class offered was miraculous, and I can't say how it began. I certainly wasn't involved, though I enjoyed the rebellion of the group. If she'd been particularly mean, somehow the class would respond by singing out the end of her name a few syllables too long. Suddenly the group would sing, "Yes, Mrs. Shalala-la-la-la-la!" And she'd spin on her heel to see who was leading the revolt, only to find our cherubic faces pinched silent once more. She was none too quick, really. Her elaborate white hair sat atop her head in big curls that seemed a foot high. I saw a hairpin once dangling from the back of her up-do, and I watched all day to see if a curl would fall when she spun around. The tower held solid.

This is how we learn, through attention and repetition, whether the lessons are forced or passive. I fit in just fine through my elementary career—until sixth grade, when somehow I had outgrown the class again though I was younger than everyone there. How did I keep getting so big? Of course, many of the girls were taller than the boys in sixth grade, and one of the other girls was getting breasts already too. I was glad she was my friend, slender and athletic-looking though she was. How could we have such different bodies if we did almost everything together? My friend group of four ate and swam and biked and walked to and from school. Yet somehow I was different.

The doctor said I needed to lose weight and exercise. Being fat was unhealthy, he said, and so, when I was ten years old, he explained that

I simply needed willpower. I thought surely I already had it. I endured a lot with composure—no crybaby like my other friends. Composure sets one apart as mature, above ridicule. I paid attention to what was needed. I already knew I needed to be thinner and that my body, with its fat thighs, blossoming breasts, and hips was out to betray me. I took the diet sheet he handed me and applied myself. There were three pages of mimeographed instructions for how to follow a diet of 500–750 calories a day. Simple. Easy. At breakfast, 150 calories might be a hard-cooked egg and a small glass of juice. At lunch, 250 calories might be a half-sandwich with ham and cheese weighed in just the right amounts, along with an apple for dessert. A 350-calorie dinner would include a piece of fish or chicken, green beans, milk, and salad with only a tablespoon of vinaigrette dressing. I applied myself and ate only what the diet said I should, all summer long. Sometimes I was better than the diet because if eating less was virtuous, and I was in control of my appearance, I could be even more virtuous. I knew I could.

"Sometimes I don't think she eats enough protein," my mother said to the doctor who weighed me in and praised my efforts. Then he looked back at my body, still tall and thick, and he said, "Well, she's in no danger. Look at her!" He then addressed me, "Are you down around one thousand calories on most days?"

I felt insulted. He'd given me a diet for 500–750 calories a day, and I'd followed it. Steel-jawed and quiet, I said, "Five hundred."

"Well, that's probably not right," he said, "but good that you're trying!" He patted my shoulder. "You're doing great." He addressed my mother again but not her concern. "You know, to look at her, I didn't think she'd be able to do it. But she's losing weight pretty steadily." He turned to me. "Whatever you're doing, just keep it up!"

And so I learned the pleasure of virtue, even if the rewards for conformity were complex and not always forthcoming. In seventh grade, I was thin enough for size twelve jeans, practically painted on. That was the smallest I ever became, even though five hundred calories became three hundred, then fifty. Fifteen glasses of water, three pieces of gum, a mint for my worsening breath, and a piece of lettuce squirted with mustard. That was enough in a day. Fifty calories. The numbers were with me always. I studied a book of calorie contents rather than actually eating food, and people said, "Keep it up! You're looking good."

When the first all-liquid, high-nutrient diet—Cambridge—came along in the late 1970s, the doctor suggested it, despite the fact that he'd been encouraging a starvation diet for nearly a year. So I began three shakes a day. I felt gorged and happy for a while to have a bit of sugar, of sustenance. But after the first month of nothing but liquid, a cupboard full of extracts to flavor the shakes, parents and friends praising my willpower, I stopped drinking them. I stopped drinking them, one by one. First two a day, then one, then none. Less is always better.

"You can never be too rich or too thin" was the sentiment embroidered on pillows and printed on greeting cards that year. I could never be too thin. I was starting to know it was true because I had stopped eating and still had a round bottom, regularly grabbed by men who thought they were flattering me. I had round boobs and thighs like they had a mission of their own. I stopped eating entirely and never wasted away.

"You look great! Whatever you're doing, keep it up." I heard this from everyone who had known me as a younger child. I was now twelve, being molested by my stepfather and frequently harassed on the street by men who wanted sex. Or maybe they wanted control. It was hard to tell what was behind their leering. Their faces seemed more often angry than appreciative. My mother suspiciously watched me and told me I was becoming "too sexual." Appearances are important. But, honestly, I couldn't help looking sexual, and I was curious about sex besides. What was my body saying to everyone? It was intriguing, baffling, and somehow there was power in it. Why else would they be so upset by it, angry, desirous, and strange?

I stopped exercising entirely—no energy. Sunlight hurt my eyes, and headaches drove me to daily naps, sometimes three hours in an afternoon. "You look great!" I knew I needed help. But how to get it? Sometimes I responded, "I haven't eaten in forty-three days." In tenth grade, the driving and health education teacher told us that the human body could survive thirty days without food but only three days without water. I knew this wasn't true. I had survived longer and could continue.

"No one in this room has ever really been hungry," the driving teacher pronounced, and I wondered if this could be so. Was I hungry? Were other girls in the room hungry? Were boys hungry? No, we were privileged, First World brats. Our families had enough money to buy plenty of food; we had full refrigerators and steak dinners. But somehow, amid all of the plenty, some of us were expected not to eat. We were expected not to want to eat. We became lovable only by not eating.

It's not that the adults withheld food, but they made us feel bad for eating it. They wanted us to say no to food. They wanted us to deprive ourselves, and why would they want that if we were really worthwhile? It was hard to figure out as a young person. Not all kids were expected to say no to food. Most of the boys were growing, and that was a good thing. They needed to eat. A few girls were too skinny, and they needed to eat (but still be careful not to eat too much). Most girls got support, got love if they were being virtuous, and so the adults supported us by encouraging us not to eat. Some girls, like me, were never lovable when we were eating. We were already too large, already a problem to be solved. Even if we were hungry and the kitchen was full, even if everyone was eating together, even if a family member made something we loved, in order to *show* love, we were supposed to not eat it.

People looked at me with pity when it was clear that I was left out of all the deliciousness and kindness and collaboration and community and belonging and satisfaction involved in eating. And then they'd tell me how good I was being when I was starving. "You look great!" People said it, and I'd respond with something morose. "Well, I'm dying." The speaker would look nervous or act like I was joking. With a smile, the person would say, "Wow. Well, you look great. Keep it up!"

Those grim comebacks were my first experiments in using my voice to state the truth of my experience. I couldn't say much, but the responses helped me understand the world I was in. It's hard to make sense of it all when you're young, but those comebacks, simple statements that I was starving, left no ambiguity. I lived in a world that did not love my body.

And the shame. Oh, the shame of being wrong, all the time wrong, impossible to erase the wrong-bodied-ness that you express everywhere you go. Hide yourself. Don't move. Don't dress flashy. Don't be loud. No one wants to hear you. No one respects you. No one will ever respect you.

Little by little, my body began offering its own counter-narratives. I learned that this body wants to live and would not let me kill it with misinformed virtue. My voice, when I was able to use it, caused a vibration in my body that made me feel connected to the universe itself. It was like being part of a choir only I could hear when I took a full breath and spoke of my experience. I learned that there is no substitute for voice. Not even observation and compliance. I learned that deciding not to move and sweat and enjoy the outdoors makes you feel like you want to die, even when the body refuses to let you go.

This was my childhood. It's where I come from. My stepfather sexually abused me regularly from age twelve to fourteen, and I remained compliant, cool, and competent.

I had my first consensual sexual relationship at age fourteen, and suddenly—through my own erotic urge—I knew that I had a greater power within me than could ever be diminished by the judgment of others. We fell in love and ate pizza and vegetables and turkey dinners standing in front of the refrigerator wrapped in blankets after sex, licking mayonnaise off each other's fingers. I saved my life by taking a lover. The love didn't last more than a year, but I did. And the power my body discovered began moving into every cell of my being. I looked like sex, walking down the street. No way around it—and sexual urges became part of how I found a home in my body. At fourteen, I left home and gained a hundred pounds over the following year. I was eating, and the weight just came, quickly. I found a voice and a sense of purpose—it's hard to explain the conviction really. Somehow I was important to the world. I knew it unequivocally. At seventeen, I found movement again, rhythm and sweat and the joy of a heart-pounding workout. I still felt virtuous when not eating and sometimes relapsed into old behavior, on and off, for a few more years. Keeping up appearances still seemed important, as was the performance of virtue. At twenty-five, I stopped dieting forever. I started the lifelong process of accepting how I look and eventually celebrating survival in a body that many disdain. My appearance provokes both joy and disgust in others—that's still true— and now it rarely provokes shame in me. I am what I am, every day, every breath; I become a new version of myself. Others still affect me, but I define myself. My dignity is inviolable.

I stopped dieting and started just living. I now maintain the appearance of a person who lives and breathes and moves and makes love. I think all of that is visible on me even now, at middle age. Maintaining appearances is important because it helps others know that they can find a home in their bodies too. My body was trying to tell me that it was my ally all along. I was simply mistaken when I tried to starve it into compliance. I forgive my mistakes, other's mistakes. Appearances matter. That's why I keep showing up.

2.

LANGUAGE, FAT, AND CAUSATION

These are facts: my Body Mass Index (BMI) is over 40. This is the highest classification of the BMI, level-three obesity. Those who use this scale call me "morbidly obese." In my culture, I am embodied as something morbid. How easy it was for language to take my life and turn it toward death and disease. And it's not so easy to re-language myself back into full life. Let me bring this to the level of sensation. When I type or say that I am morbidly obese, something occurs in my body that was not happening just a moment before. My pulse quickens, and my head throbs. Sometimes I feel panic and want to cry. I feel like I need to take a deep breath, clear my lungs. I have been handling the themes and language of embodiment for decades, and this is still my experience with the language. It's not like I'm dealing with a sudden diagnosis that brings a fear of the unknown. It's not like when someone says, "You have cancer." There is no disease in my body, no illness, yet, according to the BMI, my existence is morbid. This statement is brought to describe an everyday experience in a body that lives and acts and makes love and experiences joy. My body, that lives and acts and makes love and experiences joy, in simple, everyday ways, is labeled "morbidly obese." I'm affected by this classification and language, and I carry the classification in the body. I feel my stress level increase just so I can tell you this—there will be effort involved in bringing this anxiety back to neutral.

There is nothing neutral about being fat in America.

It's great that we want to talk about health, but we dwell on things that may be germane, but not causal. Let me say this another way. Numbers may be factual and still not tell the truth. We are not separate from the social sea in which we swim. Physical outcomes cannot be isolated to bodily circumstances alone. The stress of ridicule, exclusion, underemployment, diminished dating ability, and lessened respect are external forces that influence physical outcomes. Stress is culturally assigned based on appearance and especially vicious if one's physical appearance is deemed to be one's own fault.

I am walking up a hill a few paces behind my best friend. We are teenagers coming home late from a party. It's ten past ten in the evening, and we are walking back to her house where I will stay the night. Our curfew is ten, and she picks up her pace to one I can't match. This is not the first time she has done this, nor will it be the last. She often walks at a formidable speed. I am working to match her stride, but my feet hurt, and I'm tired. I wonder, as I have always wondered, if this is simply the pain I deserve for being too fat, for not exercising more. I want to keep up, and I am simultaneously angry at this desire. She should respect me and my limitations. I am sweating out this anger. Is it excess sweat because fat people sweat more? Or is it because I am unfit or because I am angry, anxious? And then, as she leaves me behind, turns the corner ahead of me for the final quarter-mile home, I am also afraid. It's ten past ten, and it's dark, and, before she left me behind, she said she wanted to honor her mother's request that she be on time. And off she went, sort of trotting along the dark street. Perhaps I could keep up, but I don't even try now. I am seething with anger at this stupidity, this humiliation, and the fear that some ill could befall me, alone, in a military-base part of town. I want to be as brave as she, but I also think she is stupid. Why would her mother prefer her arriving home alone at ten past ten rather than the pair of us arriving with apologies at ten twenty? But I am also not sure whether I deserve humiliation. I steel my demeanor and decide that I will not accept humiliation, whether or not I deserve it. In those last five minutes of the walk, I consciously slow my breathing and work on the comments that will let me save face upon entry, the comments that will reconstruct a sturdier self-image, one that is not worthy of derision, of being left behind.

When I come into the house, sweaty, seething angrily behind a cool exterior, there sits my friend, leafing through a magazine on the sofa. Her mother sits nearby. Do I imagine a look of irritation on her face for my tardiness? Does her mother think it strange that we didn't come in together? I don't know, and I don't show my feelings. I hide them, as practiced, and deliver the lines I've constructed in the dramaturgy of social life. I take the role I've been handed and play it as best I can, as all young people do. I will discuss a lot of life's joys and pains with my best friend, but not this one. She is one of the unwitting perpetrators of oppression in this regard. And I know she loves me. No, I won't discuss this.

The experience and effect of stress on the fat body cannot be discussed independently from the stress of social interactions while fat. Down to the subtle sanctions of one's most supportive best friends, there is stress. Does the fat person experience more discomfort during physical exertion because of the biological impact of fat on the body or because of the fear of not keeping up, being thought less than, seen poorly, fearing injury, having shoes or clothes that don't fit well or simply can never look right. How does one weigh the fear of simply not being allowed to participate with "normal" people again? Moving easily through one's day as a respectable social participant has everything to do with health.

And what happens when fear becomes experience again and again, when fear becomes memory? How does childhood memory embed itself in the cells of the stigmatized body? Being looked at, laughed at, sneered at, barely tolerated, not tolerated (and left behind).

According to the BMI, I am morbidly obese. This is a fact, though it is not necessarily true. The truth of how I inhabit this body is complex. It includes the duress of stigma and the joy of movement and creation. The research says that being too fat is unhealthy—"the research"—that unified thing that everyone quotes, sans specificity. Height-to-weight ratios can indeed serve as a proxy for body fat percentage—it's not terribly reliable in describing a person's life and health, but the process can yield data that can be factual based on specific parameters. The truth of living is complex and adaptive. I'm a storyteller in part because the truth never sits still. It dances, slumps, rolls in the dirt, and comes home after curfew. I help people understand how their particular positions and training influence what comes to be seen as truth or fiction, immutable or changeable.

Sometimes a form of hatred and scapegoating can become so imbedded in the public discourse that it becomes laudable; science seems to support it. The popularity of eugenics science comes to mind, along with the obesity epidemic as examples of how science is part of culture and vice versa. When I was a kid, I did all the same things that my slender friends did—all of them. I swam and biked and walked up hills late at night on my way home from parties. Sometimes I had a great time, though overall I resisted physical activity in the company of others. I felt fearful and pressured, and I didn't compete well. If you would argue that because I'm fat, I did not sustain the same "health benefits" from those activities that my friends did, you must be arguing that it was because of the stress of derision or other as yet uncharted factors. There was not as much joy in my walking, my bike riding, my horseplay—this I can report. I was fearful that I would not look at home in these activities, not be welcomed, and not be entitled to live a full life in the body I have. This I can report. Stress affects my body. We are never separate from the social sea in which we swim. The social world and its science are complex and intricate. We can want many things at once, and it's hard to tell what causes which outcomes. I turn to stories as one way to make sense of the world.

So how will I recover the emotional neutrality I lost when I used the language that associates my very being with death and disease? How do I move on comfortably? Fortunately, awareness of how language and derision affect well-being can itself be a call to healing. When we take the time to really hear what causes us pain and ill health and oppression, then it's much easier to know that something requires redress. That's the first step: awareness that we are living in a time of fat-hatred and that the stigmatized body requires particular care. A lot of people have stigmatized bodies—fat is just one form. People of

color, disabled people, short men, very tall women, more—all bear particular social burdens and must take care. Second, I remind myself that
the injury of stigma is not about me. It is separate from my body, my
actions, and my life. I remember that I live in a culture that does not
promote health; it promotes conformity. It's not personal. And I have
the power to promote my own health and to help others. That instantly
makes me feel more alive.

The medicine for healing stress is within us. I trust that resilience
and ingenuity are also embedded in the cells of the stigmatized person. Body awareness, conscious relaxation, and a will to help others
are powerful health-promoters. As we come together, we can remind
one another that health is also complex. We can look for and promote
healing, and we can construct systems and language that promote
understanding rather than just creating facts. And in doing so, we can
become allies. Many who look well are not healthy. We can each bring
our gifts and help each other toward greater vibrancy.

When I think back to my angry younger self trudging uphill
behind my friend that night, feeling miserable and alone, I appreciate
my teenage self most for this: she did not accept a simple story. Though
she doubted her worth, she rewrote a narrative in which her own
dignity was central. She honed her power to change perception. She
learned to level her breathing, and she continued practicing joy when
she could, without taking on negative labels as the truth of her identity. Her fortitude and *savoir faire* constructed the person I am today.
During the years that I've been telling stories—on stage and in writing—I've seen audience members access their own ingenuity simply by
reflecting on the examples I offer. I've seen others develop the ability
to rewrite their own well-being, to become positive actors in their own
health rather than victims of morbid narratives. The language we use to
describe our bodies can illuminate pathways to good or ill health. We
do well to keep looking for what serves, what heals, what connects. We
do well to name those things. And to tell the truth about them in as
many ways as we can find.

The Seattle Public Library
Northeast Branch
www.spl.org

Checked Out On: 9/19/2021 13:00
XXXXXXXXX4575

Item Title	Due Date
0010103753702	10/10/2021
After the fall : being American in the world we've made	
0010101365905	10/10/2021
Fat, pretty, and soon to be old : a makeover for self and society	

# of Items: 2

Renew items at www.spl.org/MyAccount
or 206-386-4190
Sign up for due date reminders
at www.spl.org/notifications

3.

DIAMOND JIM

When you're a kid, adult relationships are tough to figure. You just watch and listen; then you blurt out your opinions and wait for the laughter, the corrections, the stern looks. It's not all clear at first, especially with a mother. She changes around other people. My mother was so powerful when we were alone but then so different at other times—especially around men.

I remember watching the different persona she put on at the holiday parties—those were different than the fancy parties where everyone had on a more formal face. At holiday parties, everyone was dressed up, festive; the food was plentiful and exciting, but the people were relaxed. They were drinking punch and cocktails, talking like old friends. They *were* old friends, but a kid doesn't know that. There were certain people we only saw at those parties, and when you're a kid that means you've only seen them four or five times ever. It didn't occur to me that my mother had known some of those people for years. She'd had a long life before mine.

After one Christmas party, I said, "Diamond Jim *likes* you!" And my mother chuckled and said, "Who are you calling 'Diamond Jim'?"

"That's the guy with the diamond ring on his little finger," I confirmed. Most of the men didn't wear diamonds. She laughed again and said, "He doesn't *like me* like that."

But I insisted, "Yes, he does!" And she waved me off.

I saw the way he looked at her as I hung on her chair in the living room where the adults were gathered, speaking jovially to one another. I hung on the arm of her chair until the hostess sent me back to the rec room to play with the other kids. We had our own snack table and lots of decorations, and the hostess's son set up a stage with a black curtain and a record player, from which he lip-synced to *Cabaret*. They were a party-throwing family with a big house overlooking the sea. At Halloween, that same stage was central to a haunted house, but at Christmas he wore a red velvet bowtie and a green vest, and that year he was acting out *Cabaret*. My mother later said that show was "too old for me." I just thought it was boring. I liked how flamboyant that boy was, though. He was a few years older than me. I would never do that sort of thing in front of other kids. Kids were mean.

Grown-ups were interesting, and they had better food. I hung around the punch and cookies and water chestnuts wrapped in bacon. I watched Diamond Jim and my mother and the other men and women as they conducted their party. I watched and stayed quiet, in order not to be sent away sooner than necessary.

My mother was pretty but not flashy. She was classy. That's what people called her—a beautiful woman, classy. She didn't wear low-cut dresses, even at the holiday party. Her hair was short and colored in such a way that no one knew it was colored. It just looked like it was always that way: perfect. My mother rarely looked nervous, even when she was. I learned how to look closely, pay attention to different tones in her voice. I learned how see her pleasure and her displeasure—the latter being more frequent, the older I became.

Diamond Jim was smiling big at all the women at that table as I watched from the punch bowl. He stood, and they were seated at the round, fold-up table that had been brought into the living room for the party. The ladies, in their high heels and fancy clothes, were seated—five of them—with one seat free at the table. When the men visited the table, they stood and chatted—brought a new cocktail to a lady if one was required. I could have been watching any of the men, as they interacted with my mother, but Diamond Jim was big, and he smiled so broadly, and he wore a diamond ring. He caught my eye.

He seemed to look longer at my mother than at the other women. It was that prolonged gaze—just a beat or two longer than truly polite. That stare might be affection, or it might contain a drop of hostility. It was hard to tell, as a kid. Diamond Jim put his arm around my mother and squeezed her to his hip at one point—it looked a bit rough, and she laughed and pushed him off, swatting him slightly. She was smiling, though, laughing. He just walked over and squeezed her, as if they'd made an arrangement that a squeeze would be a good idea when the urge overtook him. I was starting to discern that, in the ways of men and women, this meant an affection of some kind, maybe an attraction. But it also looked like an act of dominance, to be followed by the woman's show of submission. No one acknowledged that part, though I thought it was pretty clear. All the little parts were pretty clear, but they happened too quickly to sort them out.

And my mother wanted affection from men—no, that wouldn't be right to say. She wanted men to want to give her affection; she wanted to feel attractive. How did I know this? Certainly she never said it. No one would have said it. But I saw it, clear as day. I saw it in the contentment she seemed to feel as the object of a compliment. I saw it in the way she looked with disapproval at other women being the objects of affection, being thought attractive. I saw it in the way she spoke of how some women were desperate for attention. She wanted it too but would never admit to the wanting. "Look at the way she's falling all over him. It shows no class," my mother would say when a woman and a man were standing close, speaking intimately, in a way that seemed to show affection. She wanted affection—and it was a finite commodity—but she wanted to get it the right way, the classy way. It was so complicated—tough for a kid to understand.

When my mother married her second husband, I noticed her contentment at how often he called her "a pretty girl." "Such a pretty girl." His words were like a recording being played just barely louder than the growling hostility that rumbled beneath. When he looked at other women, my mother wondered why they didn't know better—that if they acted that way, of course someone would look. When he looked at me just a beat or two too long, with the smile that seemed slightly like the bared teeth of a wild animal, she started to look at me as she had those women at the party. Why didn't I know how to act? Why didn't I cover up? Surely, I should know better. She started to wonder, how I got to be so different from her—such an exhibitionist, such a loud, defiant, willful child.

Didn't she see that I was an observer? And, as such, I was a blank slate, a curious container for the stares of others. Didn't she see that I was her daughter, her child, not more than eleven or twelve years old? She did not focus on me as a child, because I was not *only* that. I was also becoming a woman, a player in a competition for which no rules are spoken. We learn through reprimands and prizes. "You're trying to seduce my husband, aren't you?" she said to me once in private, quietly. And the absurdity of the statement rendered me guiltily mute.

But maybe I was—either trying or seducing—just by being female in the room with a man. Maybe she was right about me and everything I was, everything I could be. I tried on the possibility of becoming the tightly buttoned victim of stares I did not invite. But that seemed like a lie, and I'd also been taught not to lie. "Pretty is as pretty does." That's what my grandmother said, and there's a virtue in keeping pretty. It's so complicated. It's so hard to figure out when you're young.

And it's still a puzzle throughout life too—one we never quite solve. There's always a piece or two missing under the rug, a piece or two swallowed by the family pet. There's always a willful sabotage—somehow, someone seated at the table is to blame. The men at the party never sat with the women. That much, I observed for certain. Maybe briefly, during the meal, they sat with their turkey and green beans, rolls perched on the edges of Styrofoam plates. But then they were up again, smoking on the porch, chatting with one another, on the sofa in front of the television. There's a puzzle on the table we never quite solve.

At seventy-three, my mother started dating again. Her third husband dead, she was seeing someone who lavished her with compliments. She was still beautiful, still proper, still classy and well-dressed. This new male attention brought her contentment, but it also seemed to make her nervous—as nervous as I remembered her being when she was middle-aged and I began to look like a woman, still a child. She had become nervous again and seemed on the lookout always—on the lookout for someone's wrongdoing, a misstep that would explain whatever misfortune she endured. When I was first about to meet her new beau, a man of eighty-nine years, clearly smitten with her, she examined my blouse, and her expression judged it untoward. She said, "You're going to try to seduce him, aren't you?" And this time, I was not mute with shock. I was surprised and wounded, thrown back into an earlier part of myself that was astonished by what I was beginning to discern as the rules of men and women. Even as an adult, long practiced at paying attention, watching out for my safety and choosing carefully who I would be, I was jarred by her question. My adult voice came forth with humor, even though this was not joke. "Oh, mother, that's just what I'm going to do! How ridiculous." And I laughed.

And then she laughed. She repeated the sentiment, "Yes, that would be ridiculous."

4.

WANTED: FAT GIRL

Maybe I bumped her elbow. It could have been something as simple as that: the catalyst. And when she turned around to see me, her response was habitual—not calculated. She saw my face and then looked down my body and back up again with disdain, then disgust, and then she finished with a small laugh of gleeful pity. The entire assessment and pronouncement lasted a full second—not more than two.

Could I have imagined the disdain, or had there been some past interaction between us to prompt her disrespect? No, I am anonymous—and I have spent a lifetime cataloging glances such as these. I know the difference between a pullback that implies I'm taking too much space and a step-aside that extends respect for someone who needs to walk past. I've been thinner too, and I know that, for thin women, there are different glances (but that's another story). Those who don't experience them often dismiss the social sanctions that take place in mere moments. Perhaps they are imaginary, a symptom of paranoia. To those who know them, they are as real as the furniture.

To be fair, she had been drinking. It was late at night, and I was on her turf. That is, anyplace where the body is put into motion. I can sometimes get her respect in the classroom, or behind a desk, a place where my body is secondary to my mind. The hour and alcohol would make her drop the decorum she might use at, say, the post office. She would note my body shape and size, attire, and demeanor at the post office too, but the schoolgirl glee at my perceived defeat is reserved for late-night encounters, times of slight intoxication. For a place where she believes I am unarmed, unwelcome.

We had just left the dance floor, and I think I bumped her arm. We'd been out dancing, and the music was ending for the night. We were coming back to ourselves—the selves that were no longer ecstatically moving, bodies pulsing rhythm. We were coming back to the selves that have to find meaning in our own lives, make decisions about who we are, how we project ourselves onto the bright canvas of culture. The bracketed existence of dance floor anonymity was finished. And though I didn't know the woman who gave me the look, I knew how much she needed me.

What causes one to disdain another and think it is warranted? The fact that it will be excused, or even lauded, for starters. What causes a person to dismiss the humanity of another? A need to elevate oneself in a social order where most of us help ensure that some can be disdained in order that we may flourish. And that's why the slender girl on the dance floor needed me to be fat. While she thought she didn't want me around, she wouldn't have known how to live without me. And her relief that she could have been me, but wasn't, spurred the gleeful chuckle of dismissal to her affront. I gave her life authenticity.

By the bar, late at night—this was not the time for conversation, but I caught her eye and looked for a moment with real compassion. This did not even take a second, maybe half a beat. I was so out of place in this interaction, not doing my job. And, indeed, I know how to do my job: to avert my eyes and show the shame that I feel. I felt it as a child and still do at times when someone like her catches me unaware: the shame of forgetting that I am not credible, followed by the hot rage of injustice. But not that time, and less often, the older I get. I just looked at her with compassion—so different from pity. I was not afraid that I could've been her. I accept that I could have been her. I might ridicule another in order to elevate myself. Of course, I could. And I knew that my ability to practice kindness toward her would help us both—and probably others whom we hadn't even met.

I just stood and stared at her, thinking: I know how much you need me. Without me, you'd have to do something with your life in order to feel good about yourself. You couldn't just gloat about not being me. You couldn't use me as the ballast that keeps your head from floating away thinking of all of those on the dance floor who are prettier or thinner or shapelier than you. Without me, you'd have to make someone else your scapegoat, and it might not be so easy, if there weren't obvious physical criteria involved. You'd have to replace me or focus on who you wanted to be within yourself—not just in comparison to others.

I wanted to ask the kind of rhetorical questions that prompt reflection in a quiet moment: What must you think of yourself to elevate the size and shape of your body—perhaps what you do to make it so—to virtue? How little must you think of yourself to look at me that way and take pleasure in it?

But she didn't know me at all. Did my demeanor say it? Did she sense me thinking, "Maybe you didn't know, but any fat woman you meet has character and fortitude to spare for surviving a world that uses her as you've just used me"? Fat people may scapegoat others to find their self-worth, surely. If she thought she was so different than me, then she didn't know me at all.

I didn't say any of that, but, for our similarities, I seemed to know something she didn't. She didn't actually need to *do* anything in order to be worthy of respect and positive attention in the world, and neither did I. We were already fine people, just as we were. Even as she put me down, she did not deserve my put-down. How much lower can we agree to feel? No lower. No more.

I didn't speak at all, standing on the edge of the dance floor, late at night. But if I correctly read her painful need in her quick behavior, perhaps she read my truth in a simple stare as well. Perhaps she heard me say: "Gentle, darling. No one deserves your derision. Not even you."

5.

DANCES WITH LIGHT

When I was six years old, my mother had my hair cut in a style she called a "pageboy." I didn't know what that meant, but it had the word "boy" in it and that's exactly what strangers started calling me. I was big for my age and chubby, and my facial features were bold, as they are now. Not masculine, but bold and expressive. Long hair adds gender clarity. It can soften or reveal a face that shows emotions readily. I rejected cleverly named haircuts afterward when my mother suggested them, and my hair became a long ponytail once more.

Through my whole life, my mother's hair was short—always fashionable, but short. She wore it dark when I was a child, and the sides came into cute little curls pointing toward her dimples, not as short as a pixie cut but the same shape. It lightened as she aged and morphed along with fashion. The length of my hair was always a point of contention between us after I became old enough to refuse the haircuts she wanted. I know she influenced the stylist because it always ended up shorter than I wanted. "Shoulder-length is still long," she'd chirp. "But it looks so much better shorter! I don't understand why you don't believe me!"

In this case, she was offering advice counter to popular fashion opinion. And she definitely understood popular fashion. This was so confusing, and I thought she'd have been as ashamed as I was of the gender confusion my shorter hair caused. But perhaps she didn't hear it as much as I did, from people like bus drivers, kids at school, and shopkeepers. None of her friends would have called me a boy. Is it possible that she didn't want me to look feminine, cute, and fashionable? I couldn't imagine that. It always seemed so important to her that I lose weight so that I could be exactly those things.

If it was going to be long, she wanted my hair pulled back in clips or a bun. The bun is how she styled it when I was a small child, before the pageboy. I rode the bus home from school, and the assigned seating placed me in front of two older boys who pulled out my hair pins one by one on the way home so that I always arrived in a tangle thanks to the breeze through the window. I told her it wasn't my fault, but there I sat, as soon as I got home, being pulled by the brush, like punishment.

By the time I was eight, if I wore my hair down, she'd look at me and say, "Ew, why do you want all of that stringy hair hanging all around you. It looks like witchy-poo." Sometimes she'd try to enlist others to reinforce her disdain of my long hair. Often they'd diplomatically mention their fondness for fashionable short cuts. Sometimes, they'd actually say, "Oh, I don't know. She has beautiful hair."

I had beautiful hair, soft and shiny, and its chestnut color in my early childhood darkened to sable in elementary school. Perhaps she didn't like that I had darker hair and complexion than she did, more like my father, who was of dubious ethnic and racial origins. Whiteness was important; my father performed it well, and it's what I learned too.

I thought I had beautiful hair. I wasn't sure, because I valued her opinion on appearance. Modeling and fashion were her business, after all, and I knew she was skilled from the way others were always impressed with her looks. But regarding my hair, she seemed to be lying to me somehow.

One time, instead of the witchy-poo comment, she said something I didn't understand at all and needed to ask about. I had styled my hair, which I didn't usually do, used the curling iron and tried to fluff it a bit, though it was naturally very straight. She saw it and said, "My god, you look like a teenage thyroid case!" I was probably nine, not a teenager, and what did that thyroid comment mean? It was embarrassing to ask that an insult be explained, but I couldn't bear not to know what she was saying about me. "It just makes your face look full," she explained with pity in her voice. "It makes you look fatter than you are, and remember: everything you wear should give a slimming appearance." This was just something that had to be done. If there was a figure flaw, it should be corrected through clothing. Only use hairstyles to enhance the shape of the face; only choose colors that flatter. Learning the rules of fashion was very important in my upbringing.

That "teenage thyroid case" comment stayed with me. It seemed such an elaborate thing to say to make a simple point. She always said she was just being helpful, and I believed her. I continued to believe her against all reason. Was she trying to save me from ridicule? Did she not want me to look pretty? What on earth did she have against my hair?

Just after my very first haircut, when I was three, my mother gathered up the little wisps—they were about five inches long—fine baby hair that had actually spent time in her womb. She tied each small bundle in a red ribbon and sent one each to my grandparents as a memento of my youth. My father still had one, in his dark wooden box of special things, when he died. It rested among the cufflinks. As a child, I found this particular wisp in its red ribbon. Even then, I recognized the tiny package as a souvenir of my innocence. She didn't always hate my hair.

When I teach at the university about gender in pop culture and the media, we do a whole week of study about hair, called Hirsute Hegemonies. We analyze representations of women's hair across races. We read qualitative research documenting what women's hair means to them and how they use it to invoke privilege, membership in certain groups, and sexuality, and as an apologetic for other shortcomings. We watch Chris Rock's film *Good Hair* and speculate about whether Beyoncé could have become as famous with her hair natural, nappy, or in dreads. We always have astonishing conversations in class because all women report complex—often fraught—relationships with their hair, and many of them previously believed that they were alone in those feelings of discomfort. We talk about men's hair too, though the fear of losing it is so much more simplistic in comparison. The men in those classes are often astonished at how important hair is to women, just as the white students are often astonished at how much money black women in particular spend on straight hair and what role that straight hair plays in their perceptions of beauty.

My friend Sonya Renee Taylor is the founder of an organization called The Body Is Not an Apology (thebodyisnotanapology.com). She had worn wigs most of her life, as many other African American women do. Her own hair was sparse from years of damage, and, as with many profound forms of activism, her movement began with herself. She decided to reclaim her ability to be beautiful, wig-free, and shaved her head. Since that first radical act, she has also worn her partial head of hair, as it naturally grows in. Her heroic effort in self-love and reclamation was indeed touching to me and to many others. In the years that followed that act of self-rescue, The Body Is Not an Apology has flourished. She has published a book for adults and one for girls as well—all in the service of helping others commit to radical self-love too.

Why did my mother want so badly to keep my hair short or contained? How did it offend her so greatly that she frequently made a face or comments when she saw it—when she saw me? At age forty-one, I cut my hair shorter than it had ever been since the pageboy. I wanted to see how I would feel about my own hair-attachment. As an adult, I had always worn my hair long, often curled and, wow, in pictures of myself, particularly in my thirties, my hair and fingernails were magnificent, lush, long, and enviable. At forty-one, I cut off a foot of it, leaving it just above shoulder-level. It was nothing like a buzz-cut, and my body now reads as undeniably female. Even the boldness of my facial features no longer causes confusion. My mother loved the haircut. She had changed her tactics when I reached adulthood. The witchy-poo comments were gone, but she had occasionally pointed out that I was too old for long hair. "You're a mother now. What does a woman your age need with all of that long hair?" She asked me this, as though hair was a way to snare a mate and I was beyond the need for that.

When I cut my hair, my mother was pleased, but the onslaught of comments from others began. First came the shocked dismay—no, let me say whining—from women I've dated. Yes, dated—past tense. They came out of the woodwork at the news (thanks to website and Facebook photos). "I heard you'd . . . I mean, what did you *do*?" It's like they couldn't bring themselves to say it. These were people who'd had an intimate relationship with my hair, I reasoned. But the comments didn't stop there. On the campus where I teach, the barrage continued. Students are definitely not intimates, but they somehow feel that professors are public property. We are entitled to their opinions.

"Professor, what did you do to your hair?"

The answer seemed too simple. "I cut it."

"But, why'd you do that? You had great hair!"

That was the general consensus of family, friends, and students. I had great hair. Is it therefore a public service that I maintain it at a certain length? I pondered this possibility—that I did something to my personal appearance that actually had community importance. Or maybe as a fat, middle-aged woman I was expected to hold on to any positive physical attributes I had. Perhaps my hairstyle also has significance to my identity as a queer femme woman. It's possible for all of these things to be true at once, in varying degrees. We often hold multiple and conflicting objectives when it comes to beauty.

My stepfather warned me about lesbians when I was an adolescent. "They're so forceful and unattractive with that cropped hair and mannish walk," he said. "They'll be interested in you—but they'll want to do things that are unnatural, kind of disgusting," he added with a frown. "They don't even shave," he concluded.

I was already having a sexual relationship with a woman, which is perhaps what prompted his desire to share his views on the matter. My lover and I had never been overtly affectionate in his presence, but I think it suddenly occurred to him that I might prompt attention from women "like that." Through no fault or desire of my own, of course, I would bring something out in her.

He was right—thank goodness. And though he didn't fully articulate his meaning, so much of his warning focused on lesbian hair. Short hair on the head and untamed hair on the legs and armpits signified a rejection of feminine norms. There was something wrong with women whose hair was not controlled by convention, by a sense of presentation for the male gaze. In point of fact, that first lover of mine shaved her legs and armpits, though she kept the hair on her head short. She enjoyed my feminine conformity too. My leg hair and arm hair were shorn to her preference through the relationship. But then, I was a different type of lesbian than she.

The comments continued for weeks, from my students, people I saw at the post office, people at exercise class. Sure, hair is an element of femininity controlled as a presentation for the male gaze, and it's also something more. Long hair is beautiful—it shines in the sun and dances with light in such intimacy. It's soft and flows like water over skin if it's straight; it stands ebullient if it's curly. Even people who don't touch and experience beautiful hair directly are able to benefit from it. As Maya Angelou said in Chris Rock's film, "A woman's hair is her crowning glory."

The woman with long hair is carrying an important connection with the feminine—one that may be all the more important now that our culture has maligned so much of femininity; we need to hold onto what we can. There's precious little left of the feminine in which it's safe to revel—truly comfortable to love. Long hair is a pleasure and can be an intimate gift. Some cultures view hair as a form of spiritual offering. It can represent an indulgence or effacement of the ego. Both men and women shave their heads to show devotion. In other traditions a woman can give her hair as an offering of value; it can be kept on the altar as a thing of beauty, a tithe. It's socially, personally, and spiritually significant—a woman's hair that is long and beautiful whether it hangs in tendrils, sweeps around her body with vivacious movement, stands up on its own, or weaves itself together into vibrant locks. Men's long hair can also be lovely—and it doesn't have the same representational power. It can represent youth and virility, along with many other cultural markers. I try not to make light of the experiences people have with my hair. All of this can be true, and having long or short hair still shouldn't feel obligatory.

As she ages, my mother more frequently tells stories of her younger life. She is also more forgetful about everything recent. She was thirty-one when I was born, so there's a lot to remember before my birth. Recently she told me how beautiful her hair was when she was young. She said she wore it long, always pulled up into a French twist. I had never seen a picture of my mother with long hair, which is unusual because those were her modeling years. I can't think of even one picture.

"I never knew that," I said to her and then queried further. "You had long hair, but you never wore it down?"

"That French twist looked so sophisticated!" she replied, recalling her tresses. And then her face grew troubled. "One time, I wore it down, with a little curl in it. It fell all around my shoulders, and I thought it looked so great. I was going to meet a man I had been dating, someone I really liked, and men usually like long hair loose. When I arrived he looked horrified, and the first thing he said was, 'Look at your hair! You look like a teenage thyroid case. Put it back up.' It really hurt my feelings."

She didn't seem to have any recollection of saying the same thing to me as a child. I nodded and said, "I'll bet it did. That's a terrible thing to say to someone."

"That French twist was so sophisticated," she repeated. And then she added, "We didn't stay together, of course. And I cut my hair short soon after that. I guess he was entitled to his opinion, but you're right, that's a terrible thing to say to anyone."

6.

THIGHS AND FREEDOM

The flesh on the inside of my thigh has developed an old-person feel to it.

This is TMI. I can't help it because I'm discussing the flesh on the inside of my thigh, and that invokes an image of the intimacy I have with the inside of my thigh. I do indeed know that area of my body intimately. I like to put my hands there for warmth and comfort when I'm lying on my side in bed at night—you know, among other things you were already thinking.

That was when I felt it. The bit of flesh on the inside of my left thigh sort of dropped into my hand differently than it had before. It felt sort of not attached, only totally still attached. Suddenly the flesh on the inside of my thigh was . . . freer. Yes, that's it, my flesh was developing a freedom of form accompanied by tenacity, and I noted a new wit developing there too. As the flesh dropped into my hand, and I said, "Wh-what?" It said, "Aw, you noticed. Well of course you did"—in a sultry tone that poked fun at the frequency of my hands between my thighs.

I noticed the same quality of flesh on the back of my ex's arm, just above the elbow, the other day when we went out to dinner. That is to say, she had come to visit and brought her tools because I always need things fixed (and this is not sexual innuendo, like you might imagine). She may be an ex, but she's also a friend and someone who likes me. She charges me handy-babe prices for working through my honey-do list because she's not my honey anymore.

So, it wasn't exactly during dinner that I noticed her old-person skin. It was while her arm was moving. That's when a person really gets a full sense of this skin revolution. In movement. I saw it while she was fixing my little nightstand, had it up on the counter, and her hand was working the screwdriver, and the back of her arm quivered differently than I had seen before. We were together a decade, and I have watched the way the muscles, skin, and sinews of her arms move so many times when she is engaged in tasks that require both manual dexterity and a little muscle. Oh, with pleasure have I watched that stretch of skin between fingers and shoulder, the way her somewhat scarred forearms look in many different qualities of light. She's always been thin and wiry and, as such, had a very contained look about her. And suddenly, right there on the back of her arm, above the elbow, something was less restrained than it had been before. Less composed than in the past.

What do sixty years look like on a body? What do fifty years look like? My mother is in her eighties, and I look at her body, but she doesn't let me see much. She has always covered the parts she doesn't like. I watch the side of her neck, the only place I can see any skin movement. But then, I have never been allowed to know my mother's body, so comparisons are harder over time. I want to know myself and my loved ones. I want to know strangers' bodies on the street, people I pass with but a nod of human recognition. I want to know even strangers' bodies better than I have been allowed to know my mother's body. There is something lost in the constant quest to look nice. And it's not just a personal relationship with oneself.

Let me tell you something about being young and fat. That shit's hot. I seriously don't know how we became unable to see that, as a culture. Somehow, we took on the shame of the "bad body" invented by advertising, the shame of being "uncivilized" that fat bodies were made to carry, in large part due to racism—a need to distance slender white femininity from every other kind. Those divisions took over the biological urge to feel softness, see sloping shapes, feel the way flesh can press against you in an embrace like you'll survive any cold or hunger the world has to give. I mean, we continue to idolize big boobs on a woman, and that's fat. But the rest of the body is supposed to stand vertical to the earth like a skewer. I don't hate body modifications on principle, but that skinny child-body-with-giant-boob thing we invented is a sign of trouble for everyone, women especially.

Sure, the skin is doing a different job in its twenties than it does in any other decade. There's newness in the air around a fleshy belly or bottom or upper arm that feels like springtime. What a tragedy that we don't enjoy all the bodies. But let me just sing the praises of this one body type: a twenty-year-old fat babe is hot like nobody's business. I didn't always let myself know it back when I was twenty and fat, because I was still trying to pare it down. My boobs always felt too bouncy, but that's a matter of genetics, isn't it? Some people's skin seems to have nowhere to go other than where it already is. Some of us are a series of moving parts. All bodies are interesting—why wouldn't they be? We're engaged in a cultural sickness that wants to see certain body types as more deserving of love and basic humanity than others. The most important thing is the experience of the body, not the appearance of the body. Imagine if we taught girls to feel it all, rather than control how it looks for others. Boys and everyone else too. Feel it all. Learn what it can do.

But no. We maintain a culture that actually distributes resources like food, shelter, and love according to appearance and inherited wealth more frequently than on any other basis. The messages of media, politics, and usually family teach that this inequity is fair if it is based somehow on the inherent worth of individuals, so we need individuals to have differing worth. Unless we are consciously creating human equity, we are participating in inequality. Even if we just feel bad about ourselves, consume media that model judgment, and gossip about how well or poorly others conform, we are doing our part to maintain division. We are creating the ideology of caste that will justify the buying and destruction we feel we must do. This is true even though all of that consuming and dividing and destroying cannot lead to lasting happiness. It does nothing to celebrate the good feeling in your body when you slide into bed to rest, or the shiver of delight when brushing your bare skin against a loved one's bare skin. It's possible to be divided, even from oneself, and believe that it makes sense to stay that way.

I'll bet it's not just my inner thigh. I'll bet that's just the part that spoke up first. My ass is probably starting to look like an old person's ass too, and, hey, I'm not old. But neither am I in control of how the skin goes. I asked my doctor to check some spots on my arms and face recently, to see if anything seemed cancer-ish. She looks about twelve, my doctor, and after a little peep through a lighted magnifying glass, she waved off my concern and said, "Nothing to worry about! Some of my older patients just call those brown spots and skin tags the 'barnacles of life.'"

I smirked and said, "Do they now, my little summer blossom?" She chuckled as if thinking I was an old weirdo and went back to studying my computerized chart.

The backs of my legs are still plump and dimpled. I wear a short skirt once in a while, so I know about that from the mirror. I usually dress with the decorum my mother taught me, though she doesn't recognize a bit of decorum in me. My body has been out of control for as long as she can remember. I'm too fat. I'm queer. Those are my main transgressions. I'm not packaged properly for the male gaze in any way that she recognizes as decorous. I suppose she also cannot see my body, just as I cannot see hers. While I long for details, she actively turns away.

There's something to be said for the reclamation of beauty—how some will decide what is beautiful on their own terms and invite others to join in via admiration of their sass and moxie. I suspect most straight people assume lesbians do this more often than we do. Mostly I see women who date women worried about exactly the same fashion-show aspects of aging that concern hetero women. Traditional beauty is a little dull, if you ask me. The verve that comes from inhabiting one's body and one's life—that's what gets me hot. Seeing a life well lived, a bit of rebellion and survival on a person, is very sexy. I mean, it's not a problem for me if someone has magazine looks as long as they have the verve, but I can just as easily get a lady boner for someone who looks like a mile of bad road if she's got moxie.

Weirdly, I have a certain love for the "rules" of fashion. It's like knowing a secret code I can tinker with, maybe rewrite so it's more interesting. When I'm not wearing a black dress with a nice cardigan to cover my ample ass, I have developed some other distinct fashion statements. Here are a few:

1) Looking like a frilly, popped-open umbrella (aka *sexy toddler-in-a-tutu with pigtails*)

2) Grand Canyon of cleavage with bright lipstick and a giant hair flower (aka *praise-be to Gaia, mother of us all*)

3) Busted-open can o' biscuits, and the dough is rising (aka *yes, I meant to buy it in that size*)

The rough truth is that it gets harder being a sassy rule-breaker as I age. I got pretty comfortable being young and fat. Now I have to get used to being old and fat. On an older woman, sometimes femme-glitter-pop looks like an attempt to hold on to youth. So, how do I make it clear that this is not what's happening for me? My ex once told me, as we passed a very wrinkled, gray-haired woman in tight spandex, high hair, and heels, that she would make sure I wasn't still dressing that way at eighty. We laughed. But upon later reflection, I hope that fancy babe knew exactly what she was doing and that someone was enjoying her for all she was worth.

My body expects to be loved. I suppose that's why it talks back a bit. I really do have a long-standing friendship with those inner thighs, even though that bit of freedom-skin surprised me. I'm glad my body communicates with me and that I've learned to listen. I'd say this body is downright cheeky, but since I've already been discussing my ass, it's probably overkill. Good job that I've grown to expect love and passion and tenderness. I want our witness of one another to breed those things. That's why I look for beauty in every body, including my own. I want our love of our own bodies to breed passionate tenderness. And, of course, I have a particular (and not always naughty) fondness for lesbian bodies. I think every act of lovemaking in which we engage is a form of unmaking patriarchy. And that's good for the whole culture. I don't intend to turn away from my increasing lack of containment.

When I put my hands between my thighs, I'm doing it for my own pleasure. I'm also doing it for the good of all living beings.

7.

BIG PEOPLE ON THE AIRPLANE

He's six foot five if he's an inch. Legs like tree trunks latch into a strong torso with muscular shoulders so wide there's no way he can stay in his own seat. A full head of tousled blonde hair and a still-boyish thirty-something face makes me smirk to think of the effort he must expend to manage an evening home alone in contemplation. But what do I know? Clearly, he spends some time at the gym. Those shoulders are so shapely; he can't miss much workout time.

It's a long flight. I look at people; I talk with people. What else is there to do? People are interesting when they're forced into close proximity, besides. I'm not the only one who thinks so—ours is a looking-at-one-another kind of culture. We imagine others' stories, experiences. We amuse ourselves with their prospective lives. Most of us don't merely imagine; we envy, we pity, we lust, we judge.

Clearly, this man's physique is a combination of genetic propensity and personal choices. His behaviors have enhanced his natural appearance, and it's caused him to not fit so well in the space that the airline has sold to him. His seatbelt fits fine, but his legs and shoulders outgrow the space—they push him into the seat next to him and into the aisle. Yet his seatmate does not seem disturbed. She seems impressed. She's an older woman who looks up at him admiringly, makes space for him so that he can be more comfortable. Flight attendants seem neither worried about the weight he adds to the aircraft nor how he inconveniences them when they go by with the cart and need to ask him each time to "watch your shoulder."

I note other people's bodies. We all do, whether we're conscious of our constant assessments or not. It's the relative privilege, merit, disdain, or hatred we give them that I find worth discussion. It's the way we bestow or revoke privilege in subtle ways, without even knowing we're doing it. Moreover, I'm interested in how privilege comes to feel normal to people—so invisible; they don't even see when others are not privileged.

I fit into the space that the airline has sold me only a little better than the handsome gentleman across the aisle from me on this flight. My hips are wide, and I'm bigger through the mid-section, so my thigh and hip touch the person next to me, just as his shoulder makes constant contact with the passenger on the other side of him. My seatbelt fits, barely. The tightness of the fit depends on the particular model of aircraft in which the airline chooses to transport us. Some are roomy as SUVs, others as cramped as sports cars. The vehicle choice and size are beyond our control, of course. We show up at the airport and get on a plane. Yet, passengers like he and I live on the edge of comfort in this type of public conveyance. We inconvenience our fellow passengers not because we want to but because of the diversity of the human body, of human choices. We inconvenience our fellow passengers because a plane ticket is one-size-fits-all. Some bodies have enough room to shift and lean sideways, to reach down for a bag, to pull a knee up to the chest for a stretch. Some bodies must sit very still and feel apologetic— or not. We inconvenience our fellow passengers through a combination of biology and personal choice.

Like the tall and shapely guy across the aisle from me, I am predisposed to physical grandness. Five nine is tall for a woman, but moreover I'm fat. My father and my grandmother were big fat folks too—along with being fit and active. To some readers, the latter will excuse my physical size, but let's say I weren't active. Would I be less deserving of comfort? Really? Would I be a less respectable human being? It's a question worth asking oneself and answering with reflection and honesty. Yes, we're a famine-proof family in a time of abundance. It's amazing to be so blessed. And, my personal choices, like those of my golden flight companion, might make me bigger than I would otherwise be. I eat chocolate every day. I eat for comfort. And so do some of my thin friends. I have a beanpole friend who can cake me under the table and never gain an ounce. Luck of the draw. We're both still fine human beings, and we deserve equal respect. If we're ever stranded on a mountaintop, my portion of the last trail mix in the backpack will last me a bit longer, that's all.

But right now, the issue is space on the airplane.

I've heard people speak ill of fat all my life. Some people say it outright; others talk about health and fitness, but they do it in a way that makes their disdain for fat people plain. Sometimes "health" is a euphemism for a standardized appearance. Plenty of trim people aren't healthy, but that can be overlooked as long as they *appear* healthy. Of course, our views on "too fat" shift with time and cultural change. For a man in this culture, though, "too muscular" is pretty much impossible. "Too tall" is reached by a negligible few. I've heard some angrily purport that fat people shouldn't fly on commercial airlines. That they're weak, lazy, inconsiderate slobs. They shouldn't be allowed to infringe on others, make the plane too heavy, and use additional fuel. Fat people shouldn't assert their right to reach their loved ones, their employment, and their vacation destinations with ease and for the same price as a smaller person pays.

Meanwhile, I have heard other passengers and flight attendants offer the hulking fellow on this flight sympathy for what he has to endure in the tiny seat that just wasn't made for someone as grand as himself. They say this with a barely perceptible admiration in their voices. They have sympathy for his endurance of this seat—the same size seat the airline sold to me. I can only assume that this is the kindness he's always received. And that he has never wondered whether he shouldn't receive it. Indeed, I think he should. He doesn't have enough space for comfort, and, goodness knows, it's never nice to be put into a position to inconvenience others involuntarily. I can only imagine that no one ever wonders if he had the courtesy to consider his immensity when he chose to spend that extra hour at the gym last week. Did he think, "Well, should I? I am going to be on a plane soon." I admit, I don't think that way either as I polish off a delicious sandwich or stir-fry. Why should we think these things? We have other matters on our minds.

And let's all remember that the airlines have other things on their minds—things other than passenger comfort. There is an industry standard, and, within that standard, the obsession is profit. That's considered healthy for a business. Some obsessions are allowable, praiseworthy even. Others, not so much. And if the airlines can encourage trim passengers to focus on the fat passenger in the next seat, then that takes the focus off how this conveyance is organized and structured—how we interact with businesses with our full personal power and integrity. The practice of focusing on the fat passenger may fuel a little animosity, a little hatred, but it won't be toward the airline—and that's good for business.

That big guy across the aisle may be a monk or a ninja or a spy rather than the hyper-privileged dandy I make him out to be. He may have a much more interesting story than I can even imagine as I sit looking at him and watching how others look at him. I'm just looking, speculating. We watch each other for amusement, after all—especially when we're in tight spaces and entertainment is scarce. Looking is one thing, but judging some people worthy of dignity and others not—that's a worry. How much space does judgment take up in your head? Here's to all of us finding more healthy pastimes—like listening and love and looking for the best in one another. No matter why we come in contact with each other, it couldn't hurt to treat everyone like they're golden.

8.

COZY OR UNCOMFORTABLE: TIGHT PUBLIC PLACES

I had a moment of judgment as I walked up the airplane aisle and saw him. I wasn't pleased to be having that feeling, and there it was—immediate and unbidden. I was concerned I'd be uncomfortable sitting next to such a big guy on the airplane. Well, it was a short flight—Hilo to Maui. No need to get fussy. Better to get friendly.

He already had the seat divider lifted, when I stowed my bag in the overhead bin. I pointed to the seat by the window and he quickly sprang to his feet to let me pass. At that point, I had only noticed his size. In memory, I see how quickly he moved to accommodate me, and how he smiled.

I put down the seat divider on my way in. It's a matter of public decorum. I don't want to make the assumption that we should be touching even though we definitely will be touching. The seat divider helps us, when we want to pretend it's not happening. It helps contain my hip, which will push against it, and the person next to me. That tiny seat divider, between two big people, is like staring up above the door in a crowded elevator. It helps you pretend you don't know what the guy next to you had for lunch because his breath is so close.

It took only a moment or two; social interactions go one way or another so quickly. He said, "Oh, no, it'll be easier if we put this up. Is that okay with you? Easier that way." He was nodding and smiling and putting the seat divider up, and I was nodding agreement and trying to push myself against the window. And he was positioning himself to wedge into the seat, find the seatbelt.

"We're two big people," I said with a chuckle, and he relaxed into the seat, into the press of my body. We were shaped differently, so we fit nicely, definitely touching, pressing, wedged in, still strangers, separate, together, no divider.

"Yeah, yeah. I always wonder how the athletes do it. Those kids at the university, they're so big, those strong guys."

I nodded. "Hawaiian Airlines is pretty good too, as the airlines go."

He said, "Yeah, yeah. I heard on Go! Airlines it's tough. I'm Kalani." He reached out his hand and we angled to shake as I introduced myself too.

I can see the judgment on my seatmate's face sometimes, especially if I'm already seated when he or she approaches. Sometimes the person is listening to headphones or thinking other thoughts, and sometimes it's clear: "Oh, shit, I have to sit next to a fat lady."

And I thought it too, consciously or not, as I approached Kalani, but what is the fear? Discomfort, of course. And when I'm the one already in the seat as my travel companion approaches, the pain is the possibility of inconveniencing someone, invoking someone's irritation just by being there.

Sometimes naming the problem helps. I know some who make jokes. My fat friend asks the flight attendant for a seat belt extender in a fully audible voice. "I'd like a seat belt extender and a *light* beer!" she declares jovially. I see others who've asked for the belt-extender so quietly I didn't even hear them. Depending on the type of aircraft, I've needed the extender too, and I try to ask in the same tone I would request a cup of water. Some flight attendants hand it off like a cup of water, no fanfare and no secrecy. Some slip it surreptitiously, like it's shameful. This seems to be their training: don't embarrass the customer.

We're going to make contact. The flight is longer than an elevator ride, so we can't just look at the numbers above the door rather than at each other. Still, there are set rituals on the airplane that help us pretend we are not in such close proximity. It's not that the contact is much less comfortable, it's that touching ruins the illusion that we are really enjoying private space. Nothing private is happening in the space the airline sells us. The fat passenger dispels the illusion, and this can cause anger—or maybe, in my case with Kalani, cause greater comfort.

He asked where I was headed, and I told him Oakland. He told me he was on his way to Las Vegas for a high school reunion. Even though he's from Hawaii, a group of five graduating years got together and planned this trip. He's retired now—thirty-eight years as a heavy machinery operator, and now he just enjoys life. He asked about my trip, how long I'd be away, and why I was going. "Oh, you're a storyteller," he said with interest. "Sounds like good work. Sounds like you're busy. That's good!" He had come to Hilo to build the Kamehameha School nearby and fell in love with the place. He just didn't go back to Oahu. I coughed a bit during our conversation; he rustled in his bag and thrust a throat lozenge into my hand. "I was coughing earlier too. Take one."

We were in contact during the short "connecting" flight. I noticed how relaxed it felt to simply accept that we were touching one another, no need for apologetic shifting, turning strangely away toward the aisle or window. No need for the isolation of a book or earphones. When we talked, we talked, and when we didn't, we just sat there, taking up space.

We talked about our kids. His oldest of three was thirty-eight and a major in the army. I smiled at the thought of Kalani starting his career with a wife and a new baby, and he told me he'd also get to see his grandson in Las Vegas—his daughter lives there too. He asked where I live, and when I said I was down Kalapana way, he said, "Ah, by Uncle Robert's?"

"One of my favorite neighbors," I replied, and he smiled.

"I take groups out at night to see the lava when it's flowing," he said. "When Puʻu ʻŌʻō gets going again, we'll be at it." I raised my eyebrows, impressed. That's a good walk and tough terrain at night.

"How long will you be in Vegas?" I asked.

"A month," he said. And, noting my surprise at the length of the visit, he added, "I play music too, so I got a lounge gig while I'm there. Sometimes I play down at Uncle Robert's—at the Kava Bar." When I asked what he played, he reported five or six different instruments.

"You may be retired from one job, but you've got a few more," I laughed.

"Yeah, yeah." He said, "I got a good busy life too. So do you. We're lucky."

"Yes, we are, Kalani," said I.

And so we traveled, on the short flight from Hilo to Maui, connecting to other destinations to do our work and share our skills. We would each sit in another plane—for many more hours. And again we would each negotiate a small space with a seatmate who might believe we're just a bit of bad luck. The fat seatmate is like the crying baby or the kicking toddler.

But sometimes I'm lucky and get a seat next to a guy like Kalani, who welcomes contact. I'm not as bold as he, but I can aspire. I do much of what he did on that flight—I smile and look for pleasant conversation. I feel entitled to be there—and often I try to take up less space. Kalani didn't try to make himself small in anticipation of my disapproval. He accepted that he was going to be touching me, that we would be sharing an experience, and his acceptance made me more comfortable. Sure, I'm a body-rights advocate, and so I was poised to appreciate his approach. It's possible others would have simply forgotten that he was a big guy. They'd have remembered him as a nice guy. I thought he was that and also a mentor. Truly, no one should feel they have to put someone else at ease. We can all be doing our own work accepting the diversity of the human body in public places—and we can darned well keep our shortcomings to ourselves. Still, Kalani's approach to proximity was a gift. As a man, he might have felt more entitled to the space, but some of that gift was cultural, I'm sure. In Hawaiian culture, influenced though it has been by colonization and religion, fat people are not generally felt to be useless, lazy, or invisible as immediately as in white North American culture.

Kalani's approach inspired me because comfort is what we lack. And it turns out that comfort isn't about having enough space in your airplane seat—that's something to take up with the airline if modifications are needed. Comfort is about ease within oneself and around strangers in public places. That includes all of the ways bodies show up with regard to size, age, skin color, gender, ability, and more. If we look closely, our discomfort on an airplane reveals something to us. We're often uncomfortable around others and with ourselves. And that can change, even if the airline doesn't sell us a bigger space in which to sit while we fly.

9.

HERE'S LOOKING AT YOU

She was checking me out. No, really, you can feel that sort of thing, right? Her gaze lingered as I walked into the yoga studio—just that split second longer than usual. She caught my eye as I rolled out my mat. She looked me up and down—quickly, not in a creepy way—and smiled broadly. Then, as I was picking up a blanket and a block, I could feel her eyes follow me.

So, was there some kind of come-on coming? A budding yoga studio romance to ensue? I can tell you from experience that this glance likely has a different origin than erotic *tapas*—and if she hadn't been looking at me, I'd have likely been looking at her, for the same reasons.

We're fat women in a fitness setting. I know the look—have experienced it for more than twenty years now at yoga studios, gyms, and aerobics classes. I'm accustomed to being looked at because I'm surprising—shocking even. I'm a large woman, and, dare I say it, relatively fit, despite being more than one hundred pounds overweight by insurance chart standards. The woman who stared and smiled? She's fit and fat too. And if she hadn't been so openly interested in looking at my body, I'd have been sneaking peeks at hers—catching glimpses of how her thighs appear in those stretch pants, how her belly or arm fat protrudes from her spandex tank top. The looking is better than the not looking, let me add. We were both at peace—happy to see each other. Sometimes a fat woman will avert her gaze from my flagrant display of largeness. It's like when a closeted gay person stays as far away from the out queers as possible. Somehow, my out fatness could out her too—as if otherwise no one would know. I can't guess what my admirer was thinking, but based on her smile I will consider her kindred. Perhaps we were having the same thought: "How wonderful! She's living her life and using her body as she chooses, despite what others might think."

Part of why we find solidarity with one another is because we're scarce—at least at swank studios like that one. When I first started practicing yoga, twenty years ago, there was a range of bodies moving—sometimes struggling—through the postures. Yoga moves seemed a little eccentric, and only the bold among us took them into daily life. Back then, I'd catch stares when practicing at the airport in hopes of finding some back ease midflight. You know, those kind of "don't look now, but there's a fat woman doing freaky stuff just over your left shoulder" stares. Sometimes I'm so outside the norm that it's hard to tell which aspect of me is being gawked at. On the other hand, I receive some glances so frequently that I could make a study.

Nowadays it's easy to recognize the yoga faithful in public places: the eagle arms in the park at noon on a Tuesday, a deliberate Uttanasana at Gate 23, the Virabhadrasana 1 on the beach. Yoga has expanded its reach, but in the process it has left some of us behind. The great adjustments, clear instructions, and careful attention to detail of the better yoga studios come with a daunting environment of fitness fanaticism. It's no mystery why these studios market to the fitness faithful. They're willing to pay for an experience where they feel supported, special, and at home.

Yes, yes, we're practicing *yoga*, so we should all just go within and release our self-judgments. Whoa, now. We're working on that, but some have a steeper climb. Or do we? Perhaps it's just easier to look comfortable when one's ego attachment is to the perfect Titibasana and the $100 recycled yak fur yoga mat. It's inevitable in a consumer culture that the people who can afford to pay a yoga teacher what she's worth will be interested in status. And "hot body," in America, definitely equates with status. Sometimes the noble fat person can sneak through—the beginner who's assumed to be fighting the good fight against flab. That person can be jovially accommodated and feel a little bit of love. But what of the average plodder who regularly practices but never looks fit? Well, sometimes it's just not comfortable, so we forfeit the group support and individual instruction offered by beautiful studios.

Even if the fat yogi persists through the initial discomfort and becomes a regular, the feeling of being an outsider can persist. If you do athletic stuff—and still remain fat—there's another layer of failure to feel in the glances of fitness-faithful onlookers. Even as a regular participant in a fitness setting, it's hard to find community. As a stranger recently said to me in a class I was attending while traveling, "Just keep coming. You'll lose the weight." Thankfully, most people keep those "helpful" comments to themselves, but I've heard similar things often enough. She was articulating the two big assumptions many people have about fat folks in a fitness setting: we're beginners at fitness, and we're there to lose weight.

And, wow, there's some sneaky circular reasoning at play there. Take a look at a gym full of hard bodies, and it's easy to assume that those people got to look that way by doing that gym stuff. People less often wonder if they've congregated, in part, because they all share a really laudable body type. It's especially comfortable to be around others who all share the same social privilege, after all. This phenomenon is more visible in the way people with race privilege or class privilege tend to congregate, for example, but body-type privilege is the same. Hard-body, slender types like to celebrate together, date, and marry one other. They discuss their righteousness and their privileges in similar company—whether or not they actually exercise more than, well, someone like me.

And that's part of why I became a yoga teacher. Let me not sound too noble here—I love teaching, I've taught a lot of things in a variety of ways for years, and teaching deepens my practice. I also have a desire to model difference—to encourage others to live fuller lives and love themselves with greater ease. And sometimes this is personally challenging in ways that it isn't for someone who looks the part, though surely self-doubt about credibility can assail anyone. I've had students at more fitness-oriented establishments see me, look aghast, and walk right out of the class. I've also subbed for classes where students have seen me and asked if it was going to be a gentle class that day. To which I used to respond, "Oh no! We're really gonna kick some ass!"

Ten years ago, I would make the effort to prove my fitness, but nowadays I just make my own offering—flawed and brilliant as it can be. (And, for pity sake, if you can't focus on your own breath and asana through a ninety-minute class that isn't what you thought you wanted—keep practicing, baby. Just keep practicing.)

We need more fat yoga teachers. And old yoga teachers and disabled yoga teachers and anyone with a different body than you think you want. That's what this mess is about, right? Most students want to think of the teacher's body as a goal, an attainable one because she got to look like that by doing this yoga thing. Well, it's not that simple, despite our desire to just pay, participate, and make it so. We want to hop on the yoga conveyor belt and plop off the end looking rested, flexing hot buns, and deserving a martini (or a piece of chocolate cake— choose your poison). The bad news—and the good news—is that living a good life is more about acceptance than it is about attainment. Sure, change is possible, but it's not always the change you were taught to believe you should want.

So, are you thinking about going to a yoga class but afraid you won't fit in? Chances are, you won't. You should still go. You and everyone else in the room will be the better for it. And if you have a body that gets stares—and not always in a good way—and you want to teach, I encourage you. It really will deepen your experience to be the one demonstrating the beauty of a regular practice. Remember: you may as well get up in front of the class to teach—they're looking at you anyway.

10.

SHADOW ON A TIGHTROPE

It happens pretty regularly. I'm not bragging; it happens. Some young person—often a woman—tells me that I've changed her life through storytelling. She says that she never thought of herself or her behavior or her identity or her body "that way" before. What's more, she's ready to think and connect and strategize with others and try to change the world. Because, hey, we're all changing the world, whether we do it consciously or not. Our lives matter. Just listening to stories about the body in culture can move us deeply. Yet, for every person who speaks up after a show or lecture, I figure there are more, like me, who will be slower to put it all together.

It's been more than thirty-five years since the publication of *Shadow on a Tightrope: Writings by Women on Fat Oppression*, edited by Lisa Schoenfielder and Barbara Wiesner, published by Aunt Lute Books in 1983.

The first copy I saw was in Poor Richard's, the used bookstore in downtown Colorado Springs where I was living in 1990, the year my son was born. I moved there with my enlisted first husband when he was stationed at Fort Carson. I finished a bachelor's degree there, left my husband, met and married the second, and had a son in Colorado Springs, all before my twenty-second birthday. While I was busy, being pregnant and nursing a baby gave me time to read. A lot. Often standing in the aisles of that very bookstore. I picked up a copy of *Shadow on a Tightrope* and sweat started to run down the back of my neck into my sweater as I read the poem, "whoever I am, I'm a fat woman."

Maybe I was overdressed. No. The body knows things the mind can't yet handle.

That's so sad, I thought. It would be so sad to feel that way, to think about oneself as being fat—like it's an identity, like it's who you are. And the sweat ran through my hair and into a rivulet in front of my left ear; the room seemed dark. That book contained a series of personal stories about experiences I shared but hadn't yet let myself know I carried. I didn't buy it. Despite having been a fat baby, a fat kid for as long as I can remember, and a fat woman despite years of teenage starvation, that book could not be about me.

I was pretty. I was sexy. I knew how to dress (even though I sometimes broke the rules). I was a good dancer, and I exercised every day. I looked at that chapter heading "I stilled the dancer in me." I felt my body putting that book back on the shelf and going on about my day. That wasn't about me, I told myself, in that way we tell ourselves lies about who we are even though the truth shines like a blinding sun.

All I could do was sweat. I began to assemble all of the strategies I used to prop up my best identities so as to never, ever be perceived as something awful and unlovable. Why would these women write about being unlovable as though it were an identity? Why would anyone tell the shame of being fat? I started to put together the individual instances of body tyranny I had endured and how I had managed that unlovable identity with charm and aplomb.

See, I wasn't one of those women who stands up in my audience after a performance and sayss out loud in front of everyone that her mind has been blown. I wasn't the one who emails the next day to say she's not sure she can go on with her previous understanding of herself now that she knows she's been made to feel so much smaller than she should. I wasn't that quick. But eventually I got there, because, once a seed is planted, the sweat and tears of the body will water it. The mind will replay what it's able to hear and piece together the rest. I didn't buy *Shadow on a Tightrope* at the used bookstore. And it changed my life nonetheless.

By the time I picked up Marilyn Wann's *Fat!So?* in 1998, every hilarious and surprising page made total sense. I was ready for that book because I'd begun to think of my own experience as both shared and political. And I'd begun to write about my experiences as an embodied person because, wow, we connect with others through storytelling, and connection is vital to a healthy life.

That's why most people say they hate fat, right? It's unhealthy. Because we are social animals, feeling ostracized causes a stress response much like the stress response of being abandoned to die. It's no small thing and has no small effect on our health. The evidence is mounting to show that the effect of fat on health is not separable from the effects of feeling shunned for being fat. In essence, research can't isolate the fat from the experience of being fat, in order to know which is causal in health concerns. That's profound—and the writers in *Shadow on a Tightrope* pretty much knew it back in 1983.

Nowadays, I not only buy books like that, I add to the conversation. I tell stories about how we construct self and identity in concert with and in spite of the cultural messages we've heard all our lives. I help people come together to discuss fat stigma and also to celebrate body diversity in its broadest sense. Make no mistake, various kinds of stigma occur against a lot of bodies in our culture. If you can't find humane representations of your body and your face in the media, I mean you. Disabled people, old people, fat people, people of color—we all face our own forms of body oppression.

When we change the way we behave and what we accept as normal, culture changes. Little by little, at first, and then in waves. (I have been writing about appearance privilege and fat stigma for two decades, for instance, but this book is finally publishable and its focus an important topic in 2019.) We raise consciousness about our experiences, and we create culture. I know because I hear the revelations in audiences at colleges, universities, theaters, and conferences. I know because I am influenced by others' stories too. After all, we are changing the world, whether we do it consciously or not. Our small lives matter, and so does our gratitude for all who came before to ease the way.

II.

COMING OUT FAT

The two of them stood in the lobby, waiting to say hello after my story-telling show was over. They were quite a buddy duo—one fast-talking, big-smiling, and full of compliments. The other quiet, arms folded across chest, an appreciative smile on her lips. The bolder one started talking first.

"That was a great show! And, omigod, you're totally sexy. I could've looked at you for hours. In fact, I'd like to look at you for a few more hours." The quiet friend nodded with a vaguely flirtatious smirk. The garrulous one continued. "So, what do you need? You need a ride? Someone to buy you drinks? You don't know anyone in this town, do you? You're just passing through doing a show, so you're gonna go out with us, right?" She looked at her friend and back at me. "You're so totally going to go out with us!"

The friend added, "It'd be great if you'd like to join us for a drink. I loved the show."

It was a pleasure to meet them, watch them, and listen to their foolishness. They'd set up the scene. I was the traveling performer, and I'd done my job telling stories about love and life and romance. They were the dandies with drink money. I was hot, and they were full of appreciation. The story only had to unfold.

I met the quiet one for lunch a few days later, and, yes, we became lovers.

This is how it starts. Something pleasurable is set in motion. I do like to be admired, to be seen as beautiful and smart and funny. Who doesn't? She was hot too. And smart and funny. The whole narrative was laid out from the first meeting.

I've been "the first" for quite a few lovers. They're thin and I'm fat, and that's new to them. When I was younger, we didn't talk about it. It's a taboo topic in modern culture. Fat is the antithesis of hot, of smart. Okay, fat can be funny, but that's not sexy. We don't go there. Besides, one tries to be gentle with a new lover's feelings, so I always wonder, when is it appropriate for me to come out as fat?

There are so many small considerations in a new dalliance—when do you share intimate things about yourself that might cause a new lover to see you differently? Once you get past the hookup, you have to find the right moment to let someone know that your dad left when you were five, that your uncle molested you, that you drink wine pretty much every night, or that you once became violent with your ex and then, wow, regretted that, so, no, really, you're never doing that kind of stuff again. Never.

When do you come out about picking your nose, wearing a wig because you're partially bald, or having the ugliest feet most people have ever seen? Seriously, there are things that might make a person question how lovable you are. Is that going too far? There are experiences and appearances that might not make you seem like an attractive mate. And no one likes to be written off by someone they really like. We want to be flattering to the people we care for, and, let's face it, we want them to hold up their end of the bargain and be the kind of people we're happy to introduce to our friends.

So, when do I come out about being fat?

What may seem obvious to anyone looking at me must be made to disappear, as if through magic, if I'm also to be thought beautiful, sexy, hot, and desirable. And so, if fat is to be discussed at all, it must become visible again. Who makes it visible—and when?

It's not like we're creating a fiction. I *am* beautiful, and it's in my best interest to be seen that way. Loads of people are nice-looking, or they can put on the pretty—wear and do and act in ways that invoke beauty. People rarely pause to think about beauty privilege in Western culture. I often say it all at once: "tall-pretty-people-privilege." When one really takes stock, it is amazingly real.

Women should be about five foot seven. Men should be about six foot one. We should all be slender, with fairly symmetrical facial features, pale skin, and flowing hair. We don't like to admit it; we like the idea that people should be valued for their talent and verve, their beautiful hearts. And this is hogwash in every quick moment and in most extended interactions too. I know about tall, pretty people privilege because I have experienced the rewards. Sometimes a person I don't even know—let's say a clerk at the post office—looks up to see me and seems mesmerized by the light in my eyes, the movement of my full lips, and the subtle way I emanate sensuality. And suddenly that person wants to be more helpful. It's no wonder women learn how to enhance this response through micro-flirtation, through cosmetics and clothing that draw attention to the features that create positive outcomes. But here's what's interesting—most people with privilege come to see it as normal, even warranted. They deserve to be treated with attentiveness and courtesy. They may not even know that less attractive people don't have the same experience.

I know what it's like to be seen as unattractive too—because I'm also fat. Nothing cancels out female beauty as quickly as being fat. For many onlookers, fat is actually proof of failure and poor moral character, in addition to causing ugliness. For some, a fat person cannot be considered attractive. No way. The two categories fat and pretty are mutually exclusive.

I have come to understand the way beauty privilege works because I have been fat and beautiful most of my life. (For short periods, I've also been somewhat smaller and found, indeed, that one can get accustomed to the reliability of beauty privilege very quickly.) This is part of what I've learned: beauty really is in the eye of the beholder, and the expectations are cultural. Some people look at me and see a pretty woman. Others look at me and see a fat lady. Both are possible. Both are cultural. And, depending on which they see, they treat me very differently. If that same postal worker looks up and sees a fat lady rather than a pretty one, there is no pleasured, mesmerized look. I am to be moved through the line as quickly as possible. That person will barely have the time to listen to my request. I'm just another annoying fixture in a tedious day. That's what lack of beauty privilege looks like. There are variations, but that is the overall effect.

So, back to sex. Of course, it happens that slender people who have never considered fat people attractive sometimes find me attractive. And I have other charms too—let me not recount them here. Suffice it to say that often enough, people think I'm hot, and I think they're hot, and we start carrying on a hot little number—I'm sure it happens this way for others too.

And sometimes I'm the first fat lover in the life of a slender person who had never considered that fat people could even be attractive—and so that person goes through some internal turmoil. Alternatively, maybe I'm not the first, and that person has been attracted to fat folks before but never gotten over the shame of prolonged or public involvement with someone many consider ugly and profoundly flawed. That person is also going through some things when we become lovers, because I'm not into being ignored. I'm into being adored. And turning down the dial on *my* sexy, vibrant entitlement is not on the agenda.

But seriously, why would a fat person have to "come out" as fat? Isn't fat obvious?

If you don't know it, I'll let you in on something: there are two worlds out there with regard to how people feel about fat. In one world—the one that controls most of the media and sells most of the products, the one that runs the politics and the public works—fat is a travesty. The very word "fat" is a terrible insult from which you protect your friends and lovers.

In another world, increasing numbers of people of all body types live happily and healthily and with minimal regard for beauty tyranny. They work and walk and swim and have sex and dance and sleep and get sick and well and love and die without organizing their lives around their hatred or suspicion or judgment of their bodies. Well, they practice living that way, at least, because the other world is tough to ignore.

In that second world, "fat" is just a description, like "tall" or "blonde" or "deaf." Fatness not inherently a problem, and it's certainly not inherently ugly or unlovable. I live mostly in that second world, but I'm super-aware of how that world is encased in the other. And because of how privilege is invisible to those who have it, it's kind of rare for thin people to participate in the world where fat is just a thing, rather than being a *terrible* thing. When thin folks do participate in that second world, usually it's because they have loved one of us deeply or because they have experienced their own body schisms with dominant culture. Maybe they are genderqueer or disabled or considered unattractive, and they've come to the place where they simply say, "Fuck your fascist beauty standards. I am all that sexy and then some!"

It's really too bad that there aren't more pretty-thin people in my world, because plenty of them hate their bodies too. In fact, most self-confident fat women have, on occasion, met thin women who are angry with them for living vibrant, relaxed lives when they struggle every day with unworthiness and body hatred. Sad but true, some body-haters just can't be happy for the rest of us. Sexy fat women are doing a public service by demonstrating another way of living and loving ourselves. We're not easy to ignore, and we're not always appreciated for our verve by those who most need help. When my thin friends struggle with body acceptance, I have compassion. My own body love isn't always easy. It's a conscious choice. I know how making that choice frees me, yet, as my body ages and changes, I have to make the choice again. Most of the time it really works.

I caught my thin lover once, scrutinizing me as I moved, nude, around our hotel room packing a suitcase. When I asked what was on her mind, she said she kept trying to find the lie in my self-acceptance. She kept looking for the truth of my body hatred but couldn't find it. She was astonished that my sense of comfort seemed real.

I've been fat and beautiful, living and practicing as I do, for long enough that I know there is a lot of potential complexity in how my lover experiences me. Indeed, I'm always re-experiencing myself through a lover. Body love in a culture of constant assault is sketchy, and I have managed it variously at different times in my life. I wonder now if my youthful tendency to be attracted to thin people reflects a desire to distance myself from oppression. Perhaps it was an internal-ized hatred whereby I couldn't find people who looked like me attrac-tive. I have lived in the different worlds myself, and I know what it's like to manage unnameable feelings.

Early in a romance, we're hyperaware, often quite sensitive to joy and pleasure, the desire for everything to go well. I manage my own feelings and some of my lover's perceptions too. There's potential for invoking the pain of body hatred, the shame of beauty failure in anyone. So when do I talk about being fat?

We have already decided that I'm hot enough that the fat can be ignored, so why re-conjure it? If I can tell that my lover is participating in that lie, it's probably because she wants to. Sometimes I even want to protect my lover from having a fat girlfriend, and so there's a double lie. At least I'm aware of the lie—but she might not be. It's not uncom-mon in our culture to lie for comfort—and to protect the comfort of loved ones. Once we start talking about fat, we're opening all of our cultural perceptions for critique, and reality could just cave in. We lie all the time! Some people have an easier time discussing the experience of being fat than others. And being fat does not automatically give one an ability to discuss fat. That's part of why couples often maintain a pact of not discussing it for years.

Couples can be really comfortable lying to protect one anoth-er's frailties. Everyone recognizes this classic exchange: "Honey, does this dress make me look fat?" "No, Darling, you never look fat." Well, sometimes Darling *is* fat. Sometimes Honey is not just avoiding con-flict. Honey is maintaining the comfort of illusion. Everywhere we have rigid standards around gender and respectable behavior; we lie in order to uphold them. Women make men feel big and strong. Men make women feel small and cute (but capable—I mean, sure, of course she's capable, other than needing her man, that is). There's no other way. Why go tearing apart the very fabric of our cultural illusions when we really just want an exciting romance, a little roll in the hay? Just let the passion unfold as passion does. We're into each other—probably for a number of subtle and overt reasons—and we both feel hot for each other. We feel hot, as lovers do, both as the object of another's lust and as the person feeling the turn-on. That's the ideal, right? Don't mess with it. Just flirt and canoodle, and eventually we're getting it on; we're in bed and it's all going well and—

Why mess it up by talking about something that makes people uncomfortable? Making someone overtly uncomfortable is not the road to mutual understanding. And that's really what I want—a lover who understands and respects my experiences. I want to be honored as both fat and beautiful, for instance, much as W. E. B. Du Bois described wanting to be honored as both African and American as a form of "double consciousness." There's dissonance in knowing that each of one's identities has something important to offer to one's community and to oneself, but one or more of these identities are rejected or derided. In a romantic relationship, I want to be known. I hope to offer respect and understanding too. After all, intimately exploring different experiences is one of the things that makes a love affair interesting. Go too far and one becomes un-relatable—too different. We constantly negotiate interpersonal comfort.

It's possible to wait too long to discuss fat—to protect each other too much. I had a whole relationship and engagement with someone once, and we never said the word "fat." We talked around it, but for my lover I was only allowed to be sexy. I was only allowed to be hot, beautiful, smart, and fun. I felt I had to protect her from some of my painful and enlightening and funny and bold and triumphant experiences, and, no matter how well everything else was going, that got lonely.

Flattering clothing aside (literally), why would I need to come out as fat if someone has seen me naked?

Oddly, that's exactly when fat-as-a-problem becomes least noticeable. When we're two people naked in bed there is no side-by-side comparison with smaller women; there are no chairs to fit into, no narrow aisles to negotiate. There's no one looking at me and my partner with the eyes of fat hatred and wondering why on earth he or she is with someone like me. Fat-as-a-problem is largely social. When we're in bed, generally things are going really well. The truth is that a wide range of bodies fit together nicely, and where there's lust, there's a way. Some body haters fixate on how difficult it would be to navigate sex with bodies of different sizes, but that's foolishness. They focus on fat people. No one ever wonders how the petite prom queen and the giant muscled football player could possibly get it on even though they are radically different in height and weight. The concern over some bodies being "too big" for sex is nothing but fat hatred looking for expression.

In my youth, I hoped to avoid discussing fat all together. When I'm the first fat lover for a thin beau, there are moments when "working it through" becomes visible. I remember back in my early twenties, noting hesitation in my lover's touch as he moved his hand across my belly. I saw an almost puzzled look on his face, and when I asked if something was wrong, he was honest. He'd never been naked with someone as fat as me. I wished I hadn't asked, because, wow, those moments are vulnerable for me too, of course. I didn't want to know, in that moment, that he was "a little freaked out" and not sure how he should feel about my belly. I remember feeling sadness and just wanting the silence that comes with the pact of beauty and attraction.

Years later, in my thirties, I felt anger when a thin lover—for whom I was the first—told me over coffee that she wasn't sure what she thought about being with someone "your size." She seemed baffled—but oh-so-entitled to explain it all to me. She found me really hot, even though I was totally big. "I mean, it's like your sexiness erases you being overweight, but then sometimes I look at you and think, wow, I don't know. You know?" I did know, but I still couldn't fathom her audacity. She added, "My friends totally know how much I'm into you, so they suggested kidnapping you for a few weeks and feeding you celery sticks, so, you know, it's not that I'm not totally hot for you. . ."

She experienced my restraint, or she'd then have been wearing that coffee we were drinking. Instead I told her she needed to work through her bullshit discrimination on her own, that it wasn't my job to enlighten her *and* to have sex with her. Furthermore, "I am *not* "overweight," I told her. "This *is* my weight." I raged for a bit and stormed off, but in the end her honesty held promise, and we had further discussion and further hot sex. Even in my forties, with a whole lot of body acceptance activism behind me, during intimate times I still felt vulnerable. Aging was adding a new threshold to my body acceptance. I want to feel lovable, beautiful, adored. I value honesty and understanding who we are, both privately and publicly.

So when do we talk about—forgive the irresistible pun—the elephant in the room? And what is the elephant?

The real problem is not so much that I'm fat as that I carry a stigmatized identity, and association will stigmatize my lover too. There's no getting around it. Sure, there are disclaimers people can make to salvage some respectable social identity. Some fat people talk about being on a diet or about how thin they used to be or about how it was the pregnancy or the injury or the illness that made them that way. Some fat people and their pseudo-defenders will highlight their super-fitness or super-fashion sense in a quest to shed some stigma, but ultimately we navigate a fat-hating culture. And some of us are fat. The problem is not what bodies do in bed. That works brilliantly—always has and always will—as long as we can let lust be the guide.

This is what we need to talk about: What does it mean to live with oppression? What does it mean to fetishize thinness (to be so attached to a certain attribute that without it no turn-on can occur)? What does it mean that we allow privilege and oppression to occur in our culture and to let it remain so profoundly invisible that we'll even collude with one another to reject reality?

And when we start asking these questions, more emerge. In what other ways do we subvert the obvious in order to not need to restructure social privilege? Does coming out as "fat" in a thin-privilege culture seem a little like coming out as "black" in a white-privilege culture, for example? Or coming out as disabled? As long as you don't talk about it, as long as you have other laudable identities to offer, the stigmatized traits might go unnoticed. (Try rereading this essay and substituting "black" for "fat" and "white" for "thin," and notice the places where this works—or doesn't work—with race too.)

These are big questions without easy answers, and once you've come to a place in your life where you start to discuss them, it's tough to go back to mindlessly cooing over each other's perfection. The desire for honesty, peace, and liberation become like a song you just can't get out of your head. We begin to notice how bodies exist in culture—and in intimate moments too. And that's why at some point I definitely bring up fatness unless my lover brings it up first.

I recently had a thin lover, and I was her first fat fling. We'd been happily rolling in the hay for a few days when I asked—with very little gravity—"Hey, have you ever been lovers with someone as fat as me?"

She said, "No."

And I replied, "How's that going for you?"

She smiled. Both of us naked in bed, she said lasciviously, "It's going pretty well." Then she added, "But, hey, I could ask you the same question. Have you ever been lovers with someone as thin as me?" She caressed her lean flank, her bony hip. "I'm a little skinnier than usual these days," she said, looking down at her own body for a moment.

I gave her the once-over, really taking in her thinness. "Maybe not," I shrugged. "It's all going really well for me too, though," I added.

We kissed. And suddenly neither of us had further interest in the conversation.

12.

MY FIRST LOVER WAS NOT A LESBIAN

One night, after we made love, she stared at the ceiling, pondering.

"At least I'm not a lesbian," she said.

I raised myself to one elbow on the bed. My skin was still sticking to her skin, the sheet tangled between us. I stared for a moment, incredulous. "Is that so?" I finally managed.

She nodded, shrugged.

"You ever been in love with a man?" I asked her.

"No."

"With a woman?"

"Sure."

"Have you ever felt really attracted to men?"

"No."

She was getting annoyed.

"Are you attracted to women?"

She glared at me.

"Take me, for example," I offered coquettishly. "I am a woman you know." I pressed myself against her and kissed her earlobe. She growled a bit, finished with my foolishness. She rolled on top of me and kissed me hard, long.

"Yes, I had noticed that," she confirmed, in a softened tone, once the kiss was finished. Her body on my body, moist thighs pressing against mine, hands holding my wrists, having pinned me for this kiss of retribution, she conceded, "Okay, so maybe I'm bisexual."

I guffawed, but then she silenced me again, in the best way she knew how. I can't say I minded the disagreement—or the resolution. But being as I am, I didn't let it go.

The next day I tried to explain to her how her standoffishness from other women appeared. Surely, I thought, I could make her see the way she signaled her queerness to others, despite her closeted ways.

"Women look at each other. We stand close to each other," I explained.

"Not straight women," she replied.

"Especially straight women," I insisted.

"Yeah, well not women like me," she said firmly.

"I think that was the point, *darling*." I rolled my eyes.

The truth is, her public distance from me made me tense. It made her tense. She tried to pass as a straight woman, and because it was stressful she just looked like an awkward dyke trying not to gawk at some woman she found attractive. If she had allowed my affection, at least she wouldn't have looked pitiful.

It was ridiculous that she thought she could pass for straight. She was tall and athletic, with a muscular female swagger—no make-up, short hair, and sensible shoes. She had a tendency to say "um-mmm" when a pretty woman walked by. This last part seemed involuntary, or she would have corrected it, I'm sure. So, instead of acting like a couple deserving of one another's affection, we acted like we were having an illicit affair. We glanced at each other playfully from across the room. We played footsies under the dinner table and flirted, with electrical distance between us. I was young, and being queer still seemed potentially dangerous to me too, though less so than it did for her. Something was different in our experiences, and I was slowly putting it together. As a girly-girl my queerness could be cute. Hers could be threatening. She knew it without knowing what she knew. And, of course, our flirtations were all the more obvious because of the tension. Inexperience made me insensitive to her troubles, but I was learning quickly. See, I can pass for straight. But she only pretended she could. She pretended that no one looked at her and thought: "Dyke." She envied my femme invisibility and angered when I refused to use it.

A person could hear this story and sympathize with my closeted darling. It's possible that the travails of the time prompted my lover's inability to claim her butchness, to claim her queerness. It wasn't as easy to live openly in 1983 as it is now. We lived in Southern California, but she had grown up in suburban Virginia—that matters too. Some might say people just weren't as evolved then in their queer consciousness. Today we can all be held to a higher standard.

Yet gay culture was already established in the eighties—gay America then was post-criminalization, post-institutionalization, post-Stonewall. But what does it matter if something exists, if you've never seen it? Gay America was an unknown destination on my map—and on hers. I was new, and while my lover could have found gay culture in 1983, she'd never looked. Why would she have? She was not a lesbian, even though she slept with women and expressed her female gender femininity-free. She knew what she was, just as sure as she knew me when she saw me—but she never named herself lesbian, gay, queer, or any other such thing.

Location and queer visibility can influence a person. While she was sixteen years my senior, she had known fewer openly gay people in her Virginia life than I had in Southern California. But then, all the gay people I knew were men: hairdressers, interior designers, and models. (Oh yes, just as you imagine, "the gays" were *everywhere*. And they were beautifully dressed—and tanned.) Gay men were fashionable, but all I ever heard of lesbians was that they were ugly, unfortunate women. They had no sense of style. Lesbians were worse than invisible in my youth; they were maligned. It's not only important to *see* queer people but also to hear positive messages about diversity.

Is it any wonder that we know what we know when we know it? History is not linear. Our collective understanding of social phenomena lurches forward and falls back again—always intersecting variously with the individual paths we tread, the ways we understand ourselves, where we grow up, and how we're taught to feel about being "other." Nowadays, queer identities have become more mainstream, so that even a person in a rural or fundamentalist Christian community may have seen "the gays" on TV or the Internet. Of course, the persistent array is not all positive.

The ready information about alternate identities multiplies, but, at the same time, representations of queerness homogenize. We become sit-com characters and news show sound bites. Femmes are the hot lesbians, the object-lesbians, the female-identified lesbians, and now we bear the burden of those identities, rather than the burden of full invisibility. I definitely feel more visible as a dyke, in my queer community, than I did thirty years ago, but no more understood by hetero culture. Butches and femmes are still the only two pop-media flavors of female queer. And butches are, well, like men. At least that's what most straight folks seem to think. We've all been simplified for public consumption. That's the error I stand most vibrantly against: I am gorgeously complex—we all are.

So, ironically, my butch lover was not a lesbian—but I was pretty sure I was. I was different—in so many ways. She was my first lover, and I stood in the bathroom the morning after we first made love, saying the word "lesbian" over and over to the mirror just to feel it, to see if it would stick. I didn't know where I would possibly find others like her—women to whom I could be *that* attracted. It took a few years to find the next one, probably because I never gave up femininity in order to be visible as queer.

Respect for complexity is still what's wanted—and it's what I work for. Part of the privilege of femme-invisibility is that I can choose when I become complex—I have slightly more control over how others perceive me. My first lover was well aware of this, and she still prefers to cultivate her own invisibility as a queer person. She and her current femme partner live in South Carolina, and they joke about how their families think it's real nice that they can live together like that, two older gals without husbands. It's real nice that the one can coach the other on proper femininity, being that she's always had a little trouble with it and all. No one focuses too closely on her lack of progress with the feminine ways. And that's how they find peace together. I'm all for peace. In my case, I find peace in queer community, by acts of service, and by celebrating complexity. I've certainly moved beyond saying the word "lesbian" to myself in the mirror. I tell stories onstage. When my son was about nine years old someone asked him what I do for a living, and after a thoughtful pause he replied, "She talks to people. She's kind of a professional lesbian."

We know what we know when we want to know it—and when it's available to know. Language, explanations, and appearances undulate and shimmer like water. The way we understand things changes. I claim the word "queer" exactly because it's complicated. My current lover, however, doesn't embrace the word "queer." She's butch. She's lesbian. She says "queer" is for younger people—or for academic types. Why would I argue that point? I may be a professional lesbian, but I certainly don't have all the answers. I just do what I can. I'm the non-threatening-looking queer—the gender-normative hottie who's aging into the gender-normative nurturing mother-type. I can be queer in a way that won't make you wince. I get it. Some femme dykes are upset by their invisibility as queer, but I accept it. I try to use it for the greater good, and I look for humor and grace in those moments when the more butch and androgynous among us make fun of my femininity. Finding respect for femininity is everyone's challenge, so I just go right on talking to people, and complicating myself right in front of them. I'm happy to be part of the queer culture that's now available in mass media and on the Internet—a culture that was only accessible through books and individual encounters thirty years ago.

It may be easier to be "gay," but it's still pretty rough to be different. Butch-femme couples like my first lover and her current partner can still cultivate a relative invisibility. It's easier because they don't use any fancy language that would make straight people uncomfortable; folks have been doing it silently for generations. They're good neighbors; whatever it is they are doing, they don't do it in the streets and scare the horses. And, at the same time, because of all the boldness that came before me, it's easier for women like me to be more visibly queer. My first lover is not a lesbian, but I am—both contrary to what people might guess before they get to know us.

13.

BECOMING TRAVOLTA

Saturday Night Fever was the first R-rated movie I ever saw. I sat uncomfortably next to my mother during the whole film, knowing that at some point someone would have sex and that she'd have her eye on me.

And there it was: John Travolta and the woman he will dump start to have sex in the back seat of a car. But I was even more uncomfortable when that young woman cried because Travolta hooked up with someone else. I could feel my mother's smugness. That trollop got her comeuppance. It was her own fault, and my mother wanted me to take a lesson. That's what I imagined anyway. Later, at home, as she was ironing and I sat on her bed, my mother wanted to know if I had any questions about such an "adult film."

Good heavens, no! Under no circumstances did I have any questions about that film. I most certainly did not. La-la-la. I tuned out whatever she said next. It was awful. The next time I saw an R-rated film with my mother was probably twenty years later, and it was only slightly less uncomfortable.

When I'm a guy in my mind's eye, I'm a young John Travolta character. I'm Vinnie Barbarino from *Welcome Back Kotter*, or I'm dancing in a white suit in *Saturday Night Fever*. Or, better yet, I'm in all black with my hair slicked back, singing "You're the One That I Want" in the final scene of *Grease*.

It's not that I'm interested in being a guy or taking on a romantic role other than my own, but Travolta was one ingredient in my adolescent stew. He's really the only male actor I've imitated with any regularity—and I became Travolta across a range of characters.

My friends and I loved the music from *Saturday Night Fever*. The Bee Gees were dreamy, and the Gibb brothers were the hotties of the day. Andy Gibb performed the first big stadium concert I ever attended. Though the film was important, not all of my friends were allowed to see it—because it was rated R—and the nightclub scene it depicted was a little complicated and disturbing for some of us. We mostly listened to the music and ignored the film. The romantic dancing was too hard to imitate anyway. We stuck with hip shaking and that diagonal, up-and-down pointing thing that Travolta did in his white suit.

When *Grease* came out a year later, however, my friends and I were in our element. Even though those actors didn't look like high school kids, we accepted them as our own. It was 1978. My friends and I ranged in age from ten to thirteen, and the plot line was easier to understand than *Saturday Night Fever*. There was no urban grit, just the silly suburban setting in which our plotlines were also played, despite the 1950s being long gone. *Grease* was a superbly satisfying love story for us. And what did we love best? The transformation of Sandra Dee.

Wow! We all wanted to be her—to have *that* kind of power over *that* kind of guy. Wow! We loved "Greased Lightning" and squirmed through "Hopelessly Devoted," waiting for it to end. But then, over and over, we'd dance and lip-sync and sometimes even sing, "You'd better shape up! 'Cause I need a man, and my heart is set on you."

The trouble with the burning need to put on this spectacle over and over again was that we were all girls. Boys had no interest in playing this game (and we'd have likely been embarrassed to ham it up around them anyway). We all wanted to be Sandy in her shiny spandex pants and stiletto heels.

But in my friend group of four, I was always cast as the leading bad-boy greaser. It was my destiny. I already knew the score and had come to embrace my role in the group. Ask anyone who grew up as a fat girl if she ever got the female lead with thinner girly girls around. I'd put money on the answer being no. This is probably also true for girls who were considered unattractive, if their prettier friends wanted those roles. We didn't even discuss it—that's just the way it was. Someone had to be Travolta, and it was going to be me. I was the biggest of the group, therefore the most convincing guy. Or maybe I was the least convincing Sandra Dee. No discussion was needed. We took our roles from Hollywood and did our best to divvy them up and act them out in our child bodies.

The leading lady role, the feminine role—playing the one to whom men *needed* to be attracted—was not for me. It's the most important lesson some girls get early on. Not everyone can try out for that part. You won't get it, and you'll only humiliate yourself trying.

Of course, it isn't actually true. Some girls learn to be pretty by reading the fashion magazines, using makeup in just the right way. Boys can be duped into thinking you're pretty if you act sexy and wear the right fashions, along with enough mascara and eyeliner. Everyone just goes along. It's different for fat girls, though. No one goes along. Boys—and men—were still attracted to me; it was just harder for them to admit it. They knew they needed glamour, and it was beyond my ken.

Glamour was the reason Sandra Dee became a knockout, after all. She was just a pretty little girl before the final transformation. She was just—nice. With her hair all curled up, wearing bright lipstick and stilettos, she became the trophy for which Travolta could openly yearn and compete.

So, over and over, my best friend and I practiced that part where Travolta falls to his knees in front of Olivia Newton John. I practiced the shoulder-leading hunch with which he follows her as she slinks away only to return and dominate him again and again. I sang, "You're the one that I want," and my other two friends added the falsetto "ooh, ooh, ooh." I practiced as my bouncy little blonde best friend—insecure in her own freckled beauty—vamped over me in an overly theatrical way, wearing her older sister's stiletto heels and ill-fitting spandex pants. The other two girls in our foursome were understudies for Olivia Newton John—sometimes they were hand-on-hip Stockard Channing just for fun. But I was Travolta.

It's not like I hadn't been prepared to take the role that supports feminine stardom. I already knew the score from being excluded from things like gymnastics class and ballet. The teachers wouldn't know what to do with a body like mine, and, besides, it would just be cruel to put a girl like me in leotards and tights to be laughed at. So I became the spotter when my friends practiced their backbends and walkover handstands, literally a supporting role. I knew how to praise their effort, to spot precision and budding talent, though never in myself. (I only learned as an adult, in my own yoga practice, that I could have done those backbends and handstands too.)

I have to admit, I adored being Travolta, though I could never take the role public in the same way my friend was actually practicing to act like sexy Sandy at parties and dances. I was doomed to be a closet Travolta, never Olivia Newton John. So much of my potential was wasted as a wallflower.

At some point I started to realize that there were more like me: fat girls who could really dance and knew what it meant to be hot—fat girls who knew how to be funny and smart. We were observers and supporters, yet we were also Travolta, the leading man, in our own minds.

At some point—not until I was an adult—I realized that being restricted by convention may have been lonely at times but that in this I was not unique. Other fat girls took their roles with zeal, all the while studying both parts with fervor. See, we didn't stop being Olivia Newton John inside, even though we had the Travolta role. Sure, some girls who grew up to identify with masculinity were probably pleased as punch to become Travolta and never gave Olivia another thought. Those are the women I date, but I wasn't one of those.

I don't know this for sure, of course, but I suspect that the masculinizing of fat girls, ugly girls, and gay girls can have a fabulous side effect. Perhaps it turns some of the queer girls into assertive femme dykes. There are more than a few of us out there—and I've always wondered how *so* many femme dykes (fat femmes in particular) can be so fabulous! It takes some gumption to be other than average in the female category (fat and queer) and to reclaim—and sometimes exaggerate—the big prize that Sandy finally held aloft in *Grease*: assertive sexy femininity.

Becoming Travolta wasn't an entirely raw deal. He was the leading man, after all. My other two friends only understudied Olivia Newton John—we *all* did that—but in the show I was the male lead, again and again. And I didn't become Danny Zuko, Travolta's character in *Grease*—I became Travolta. He's had a long and varied career with lots of different roles. Our adolescent experiences stick with us—and I could have done worse. I was lucky enough to become Travolta. Even after I was grown, some part of me still expected the leading man role. After all, I've also two-stepped with Debra Winger in *Urban Cowboy* and twisted with Uma Thurman in *Pulp Fiction*. And I was Debra. I was Uma.

Romantically, this versatility served me too. When the time came, I knew how to be hot like the leading ladies, but I also knew how to prompt my butch lover to be the best Travolta she could be. I knew it because I lived it. I didn't want to take that role, but I did it until I didn't have to anymore. Armed with Travolta-skill, I know how to prompt it in others. And for the girls who only ever wanted to be Travolta— the ones who groaned over ballet slippers for Christmas and weren't allowed to moon over their dads or brothers shaving—I am a beautiful homecoming. My butch lovers return the favor; in addition to knowing how to appreciate femininity, they also read and prompt my complexity.

Sure, it would be a better world if we all had the freedom to be all the characters we like best—one by one and in innovative combinations. I hope that day is coming. And becoming Travolta wasn't so bad. It's amazing how the roles we didn't want can make us richer sometimes.

14.

DOES THIS LIMP MAKE ME LOOK FAT?

I'm watching the door rather intently. I will raise a hand to wave as soon as I see my mother. The restaurant is busy, plenty of bustling activity around the bakery case, waitresses walking to and fro. I don't want her to fluster, there at the door, wondering where I am. One patron after another walks in. Oh, look, there's a guy in a military uniform, carrying a crutch, limping. It's the kind of crutch the doctor's office gives, not the more personalized tool a permanently disabled person might carry. I immediately wonder about his story: a sports injury perhaps, or is it combat-related? His gait is impaired, but his body remains upright, proud. The uniform aids the appearance of credibility. He may have slipped in the bathtub or gotten drunk and fallen off a curb, but these are not the first possibilities that spring to mind.

My mother finds me easily, and, as we chat over lunch, she's telling me about the man she's dating. She's known him forty years socially and as friends. Indeed, I have memories of him from my childhood. He often brought me a gift when I was very small, and one time, when I was about three years old, I acted entitled to the gift and did not thank him. When next he came, I expected another gift, and he sat down and patiently explained that I didn't seem grateful last time and so he hadn't brought me another gift. I was shaped by this lesson and remember it vividly to this day. Both my mother's husband and his wife are now deceased, and they've begun seeing each other regularly, though my mother has a hard time saying she's dating him. He says he's dating her, that she's "his girl." He compliments her beauty and likes a little kiss now and then. He's twelve years her senior and more infirm than she; he walks with a limp. His heavy body shakes with the pain of his gait.

"He's sharp as a tack," my mother says. She always points out his charm and mental acuity. She says he was never fat as a young man, that he has a glandular disorder now that makes him fat. She notes his glamorous and athletic past and then laments his decline. She is not attracted to him. At times, she makes this plain and says to me, "It's just so sad. He was such a handsome man all his life. Now this."

Because we are talking about the man's physical decline and I've just seen the service member with a crutch, I am attuned to how people limp. Indeed, over lunch, another person on crutches appears. We're dining near a university, and this one comes with foot wrapped tightly, using two crutches, wearing shorts and college T-shirt. He's lanky, strong, and sturdy. Both attire and appearance scream sports injury. He is clumsy, though, not graceful and upright like the soldier. This is incongruent with his athletic appearance, but the other cues outweigh this clumsiness. His attire and age—and the injury itself—offer a credible performance of athleticism.

It's not the body alone that tells us what to believe, though most people treat the body as a form of evidence, re-traceable to crimes and virtues. The body, along with its performance, costume, and demeanor, provide cues for social labeling. Suddenly, without even applying rational thought, we become sure of what to believe about a person.

As children and throughout our lives, we learn to ascribe meanings to bodies. As Erving Goffman's research on social stigma pointed out in *The Presentation of Self in Everyday Life* in 1956, a physical defect can cause a profound loss of social credibility. We even begin to assign character flaws to those who seem defective, unless there are saving traits, accounts that affirm a stigma-free identity. Bodies wear a limp in different ways.

A graceful countenance, good fashion sense, upright posture, and a slender face all help a person maintain a positive self-image, that's for sure. I should know, because, while fat, I possess these traits. The fashion sense is debated—by my mother in particular—but the rest seem agreed upon by most. I can sometimes be excusably fat. I am lovely and fat, charming and fat. I am smart and fat. But then there's the limp. I've had it for a few years now. First it was an athletic injury that wouldn't quite heal. It was my foot, and I didn't do well following the doctor's advice to simply "stay off of it." I switched to less vigorous workouts, but I still had trouble saying no to a nice hike, and hiking on the uneven terrain reinjured me. Then my compensation strategies caused new injuries. X-rays now show osteoarthritis. Most of the time, I walk with a limp.

Does anyone look at me and think what they think of the young college student on crutches? Or the soldier? Do they look at me, now past my forties, note my beauty, and wonder what I was like when I was young and hot? Perhaps the latter. I don't know. It's more likely they simply glance and see a fat lady with a limp. And the reason most will do this without even giving it conscious thought is that my limp is associated with fat and inactivity. I become hyper-visible—a public body. It's not just that I'm large, but people are entitled to look at me just a beat longer than is polite. Do those who glance longer than a moment give more scrutiny to what I'm eating in this restaurant? Almost certainly they do, because portion sizes and food choices are pretty universally regarded as indicators of body size and shape, despite the dearth of empirical evidence that this is not so. (That's right. Fat may not correlate directly with food consumption—and eating less does not always cause weight loss.) I already know these looks. I've been fat all of my life.

Charming, attractive, except for that limp. It draws attention to what charm conceals: the body's shape and size. Something is not moving freely, properly. And in polite society we like an even flow of movement. The incongruent gait prompts pondering. It prompts sympathy, pity, and blame. The body is not carrying the information as much as it is performing and prompting associations with virtue or evil.

It seems so long ago that Goffman told us how an identity could become permanently spoiled by such incongruities as physical defects, character defects, and membership in devalued social groups—how one trait will prompt the perception of the others. We seem so far evolved from the 1950s, yet I wonder. Are sanctions perhaps more vicious than in Goffman's time, now that the decorum not to speak ill of others has fallen partially away? Of course we still withhold privilege from those who are inexplicably uncommon, but has judgment intensified? I cannot say.

I can feel the glances on my body as I walk unevenly from our table to the bakery case and then the cash register, and I wonder. Does this limp make me look fat? Or does it couple with fat to amplify the perception that I've failed at being virtuous? Even without a uniform, I stand as tall as the soldier, holding on to my memories of a more respectable past, as I pay my bill.

15.

THE CHANCE TO PRACTICE

I've been practicing yoga for nearly thirty years, teaching for twenty. Yes, I have the body of a long-term yoga practitioner. I've done things with my body that would astound you. It's the yoga body all of the magazines have promised.

Go ahead and laugh. Because we all understand, without saying why, that no one is supposed to want a fat body like mine.

My regular yoga practice started because my back hurt from carrying the baby. My friend Wendy said, "Come with me to the adult school where I just started taking yoga twice a week. The teacher's a little weird, and it's a big drafty room with concrete floors, but maybe it'll help your back." That was when there were probably three yoga studios in San Diego, rather than three studios in every neighborhood like there are now that yoga has become a fitness craze.

We called the teacher Freaky Phyllis because yoga was a little weird and she was always saying goofy stuff about superior Hindu spirituality. She wasn't a really clear thinker, Phyllis. One day we were resting in corpse pose at the end of class, and she started talking about how Mother Teresa is a perfect example of Hindu spirituality. That I couldn't swallow, and so I popped up and said, "Phyllis, Mother Teresa is *Catholic*!" To which she clucked and said I just didn't understand.

So Wendy and I decided we couldn't stand Phyllis anymore, and we wanted to learn more, so we chose a different yoga studio, a proper yoga studio, but we couldn't get it together for our first class on the same day. Wendy went on Tuesday; I was going to go on Thursday. We'd work it out to go together the next week. Wendy reported to me that the class was great. Quiet, nice props (bolsters, mats, etc.) good instruction. So on Thursday I showed up a bit early and met the teacher. She looked me up and down and said, "Oh, I don't know if I'm going to let you come to the class tonight."

At first, I really didn't understand. Even though I've been the fattest woman in the aerobics class, in the gym, and on the trail all my life, I wasn't thinking about being different in the yoga class. The adult school class we'd been attending had a variety of students—different ages, shapes, and sizes. This new teacher looked at my body some more and said, "Well, you know, with new students, we have you take some private classes first. Then we can tell if you're able to join the group class."

"Oh, I'm not new to yoga," I said. "I've been practicing a couple of years."

To which she replied. "Well, clearly you have some orthopedic difficulties."

And so I left, my face hot with silent shame. Because she was in charge, and that's how it works.

She probably didn't even mean to be biased or bigoted or even realize she was treating me differently than slender Wendy. She was probably just managing her discomfort with my body, and her mind was super-fast to make up an excuse with which she was really comfortable. Honorable even. She was just being reasonable.

This is how it works: I'm not supposed to say anything. I was supposed to take the shame she gave me and carry it. And at that youthful point in my life, I did. I turned and left and tried not to feel bad when Wendy would mention taking classes at that pretty little studio.

Because I didn't speak up, that teacher never had a chance to practice being her better self, to confront her fears of my body. She had to keep those fears and had justified them further because I followed the script. We both followed the cultural script we were given.

But don't be sad. You know how this story ends. I found a studio that treated me like a regular student. Indeed, I became a regular student and then trained to be a teacher. And I welcome everyone to the yoga mat. I welcome bodies like mine, bodies different from mine, and some bodies that scare me too. How will I teach this person? I wonder. And then I challenge myself to learn. I check my language and how I interact with bodies, because we all deserve respect and encouragement, and my culture's failings are in me too.

When people question my body when I'm in my yoga teacher role, as they sometimes do with words or glances, I give them another chance. I smile and maintain eye contact and remain in my full humanity as they question my validity. It doesn't happen all the time, but it happens consistently. That's the culture in which we live. The fat middle-aged lady shouldn't be the fitness instructor, yoga instructor, rock climber, or disco dancer. The fat middle-aged lady shouldn't be physical or respectable in any way. I am respectable in the body I have every day, and I give people a chance to join me in that view.

I'm a yoga teacher, and I show people how to practice with the body and the mind. Just like with yoga, diligence brings improvement. It doesn't matter who we are. When we practice something often enough, we change.

16.

THE AGING YOGA BODY

Three times this week I witnessed yoga students, over age fifty, struggling into poses that likely sent them searching for the ice pack later. One man and two women. I'm guessing about their ages; saying "over fifty" is erring on the side of youth. The first student was new to my class, and based on the way she scrutinized my posture and gaped with disbelief when she couldn't do what I was doing, I would put her in the category of "people who think they're failing if the fat lady does something they can't." During my decades of yoga practice, that's become a sturdy category. And, hey, mostly I have compassion, because I used to think that way too. Our culture has taught us that bodies (and many other things too) line up along a hierarchy of worth, and fat bodies are among the most devalued. If the fat yogi or the old yogi or the disabled yogi can do something you consider "advanced," chances are, you're pretty impressed.

The man I witnessed was also straining in an easy-to-categorize way. It was a yin class. To some, this is "the easy class," and his hamstrings were tight. He resisted the props and continued struggling into the pose despite my cues to support and surrender. The two women were also struggling, though with spinal flexibility rather than hamstrings.

Of all the things I miss about youth, spinal flexibility tops the list. Honestly, it's not a huge list. I don't mind aging as much as most, but then I already have more body acceptance than most, and I'm comfortable with various countercultural views. But, wow, the spine. I can feel it when I sit too long at the computer. And then there's the osteoarthritis I've been learning to live with these past few years. I'm just over fifty.

I'm not saying I feel old. I'm just being honest here, in a useful way, about life in this body, while practicing yoga.

A lot of people stop exercising when things start to hurt too much. There are good reasons why people don't modify their activities and accept their bodies. A lot of them have to do with social privilege, avoiding humiliation, or being labeled old sooner than they'd like. So people keep trying to do the same things they've always done. They try to look the same, hide the limp. Sit up straight and soldier on. And then add on the misguided idea that yoga is supposed to keep you young forever. So what? If I'm showing signs of aging does that mean I've been doing the yoga wrong all of these years? Does it mean I'm not doing enough and I just need to push harder? What does it mean to live in the body and the mind? The real body and mind—not the ones we wish we had.

It happens to us at different times in life—some remain active with few aches and little stiffness into their sixties or seventies. Perhaps my body is developing these changes sooner because of genetics or because I'm fat or because I did high impact exercise for many years. It doesn't matter. What matters is accepting the body and using yoga and other physical practices to keep the body healthy and the mind calm.

I often tell students that yoga is for the body they have today, not the ones they had yesterday or last month or ten years ago. Not the ones they might have in three months after they work out every day, or in a year when they've lost some weight, or even in ten years when they're slowing down.

Yoga is for the body you have today. You have to pay attention to know how much it can do. Be neither precious nor reckless with the body. This is the only one with which you can practice. Take a breath. There is no other body.

There is also no other mind than the one you work with today. We live in a youth-obsessed culture. And the yoga culture we've developed as a microcosm of the broader culture is also obsessed with mystical, youth-preserving magic. Add those together and it's pretty tough to age honestly—whether the process of aging becomes noticeable at thirty or eighty. Though it is certainly possible to work toward a more compassionate ideological framing of age, it's not a pursuit one will find in most studios and gyms.

I'm not arguing against the health benefits of yoga—far from it. I'm arguing in favor of honoring the natural process of aging, of healing from injuries. I'm arguing in favor of changing how young, lean, muscular bodies are privileged above all others.

Once, when teaching an intensive inversion practice, I commented on the esoteric benefits of "taking a different view" by being upside down. I commented on how frightening inversions can be, even if the body is physically ready to support you in a pose like headstand or full arm balance. I joked about what a slow learner I am. "I was on the ten-year-plan with headstand! For the poses that challenge me, I add about one per year."

After class, a student followed up on my remark. He found his own slow progress with certain poses very discouraging. He was pleased by what I'd said but wanted clarification. "You may add one challenging pose per year, but you're over forty now, right? I mean, once you have them, you never lose them. Right?"

I was forty-two at that point. I had never considered my eventual decline in yoga that way before. Indeed, I had not yet lost the ability to do any yoga poses. But logically, I told him, if I lived long enough, I would.

I have now lost the ability to do certain poses I could previously do. And maybe I will again have the flexibility to do a drop-back backbend. Maybe it's not gone forever. But why would that be an interesting goal in my practice? As I age, it becomes more important to me not to do fancy-looking postures but to maintain daily strength, balance, and flexibility, live pain-free as much as possible, and develop an enduring partnership with my mind and body that allows me more consistent peace and happiness. Everything in the dominant culture, and media representations of women in particular, is fighting against that goal. And we do well to remember that yoga media are also largely advertising-driven. It preys on our yearning for beauty and privilege.

One of the things I appreciate most about aging is having more practice with loss and dignity, more practice with the folly of seeking privilege rather than authenticity. We can help each other remember what it means to live as allies with our bodies. And eventually our knees may start to remind us too. Our reframing of aging becomes all the more powerful when we gather with others who are also interested in body liberation—fat athletes and yogis, black qi gong practitioners and Chinese capoeira enthusiasts, geriatric hip-hop dancers and anyone who extends a sincere love of movement beyond stereotype and the desire for appearance conformity. We are here, and our ranks are growing.

17.

MIGRATION PATTERNS

My son Caleb convinced us to buy the RV. His logic was irresistible. He would sleep on the bed above the cab of the truck, so that I wouldn't have trouble climbing up and I wouldn't fall out in the middle of the night in case I sleepwalked. He would learn how to use the giant icky tube that lived inside the back bumper in order to hook up the RV to the dump station. He would wear the latex gloves in the glove box when he hooked it up and turned the switch to let all the poop fall out. He would also be the one to make sure all of the windows and top hatches were closed before we took off driving somewhere, so that nothing flew away. He would latch all of the cupboards and turn the lock on the refrigerator door to "on" so our mustard didn't squirt all over our living quarters and make a big giant mobile kitchen mess.

Really, this purchase would be 100 percent comfortable and worry-free for me. My precious six-year-old son assured me of this. My only job was to buy the RV. Surely—*surely*—I could do that one simple little thing. He said this as he danced around on the sidewalk, still wearing one purple latex glove from his lesson on hooking up the dump hose.

My girlfriend and I were already pretty sure we'd buy it—that's why we took him along on this second look, just to make sure he was into it. I really didn't want ever to touch that dump hose, so it was in my best interest to convince him that I needed convincing. And he was into it. Oh, was he into it.

During our first year of RV ownership we took the quintessential American family summer vacation: the Grand Canyon, then to the Midwest to visit my girlfriend's family. We were gone a month, and when we returned I spent two months waiting by the mail for news of my canonization for the miracle of cooking everything over hot coals for thirty days straight. There was a stove in that RV, but it was hot as Hades, and we had no air conditioner. Every time we stopped, I'd sling out the charcoal and get the fire going. I had one skillet, and my campfire repertoire was limited to veggie burgers and pancakes. Over and over and over again. After a few months with no news of sainthood, I realized that I really did want to make another trip.

During the next two years, we took a number of short trips up the California coast and one trip south to Mexico. The three of us traveled together with Caleb's dad and our other close family friend who is something of a fourth parent to Caleb. The RV can sleep three comfortably—four if we double up—and even five with a sleeping bag in the center aisle.

Sometimes our family seems exceedingly normal—almost anachronistic really, in our desire for our son to go camping and hiking and learn to work an RV dump station, in our stalwart insistence that he learn to swim, play a sport, take music lessons, and go roller-skating. He told me recently that we didn't take him to as many athletic events as his friends seem to have attended, but he's definitely seen more theater and dance performances. If I did anything right, he's watched a little less television too.

But then, to some, because our family is broader than two parents, and the genders vary, we're total freaks. Because we're queer, we're—to be redundant—odd. And not only do the genders vary, so do the gender roles. Once my son's father came over when our little boy was in the garage doing woodworking with my girlfriend. As we looked on, he quipped, hand on hip, "I'm glad you're dating someone who can teach our son to be butch." And, indeed, our son is now a competent handyman—and a competent dessert maker, thanks to his cake-decorator dad.

Some people worry that a jumbled-up family will be confusing to a child—damaging, even. Some go so far as to say that families like mine will damage our very culture. Everything will be akimbo, and our moral compasses will spin wildly, leaving children crying in the streets.

That's just not how it is. I know, because I've parented under these unique conditions. And I think most families are unique somehow—some just try to hide it. Perhaps that's more damaging to children than simply knowing what's what and who loves them and defining the terms as necessary.

On one weekend RV trip to see the monarch butterflies resting in Morro Bay, California, before they flew south to Mexico, my son's father, Richard, and my girlfriend, Katie, were both along with Caleb and me. Caleb was about seven years old. As Richard drove, the rest of us sat at the back table—Katie reading her novel, Caleb and I having light conversation. After a thoughtful moment of silence, Caleb looked at me and said, "If you're my mom, and Katie's my stepmom, and Dad's dad—and if Dad's your husband and Katie's your girlfriend—then who is Katie to Dad?"

He wasn't distressed about it, just trying to get all the titles right. I was still trying to sort out the question when Katie calmly looked up from her book and said, "That makes him my step-spouse."

"Oh!" said Caleb, with a look of satisfaction, as though that obvious detail had simply escaped him. And Katie went back to her book. Soon after, we stopped at a gas station—because those RVs really drink it down. I relayed the story to Richard, who chuckled and said, "Makes sense." And then we had a small argument with our son about why we wouldn't buy candy at the mini-mart. He didn't get M&Ms, but somehow he ended up with a lollipop. His dad's a chump that way. We got back in the RV, with me in the driver's seat, and then the three of them started a game of cards.

The monarch butterflies were beautiful that weekend—lining the trees and becoming a bright orange sunburst as they took flight. We attended a class and went on a hike offered by the natural history museum. Those butterfly migration patterns are amazing—and complex. But somehow they figure it all out. And so do we. We figure it out—like it's the most natural thing there is.

18.

THE NAKED PLACE

It's not like we went looking for the naked place. I wanted my family to be safe as the year turned from 1999 to 2000, simple as that. Some thought the world was going to end—for a variety of reasons. Some feared that the Y2K computer virus would shut down the world's computer systems, and, in the chaos, we'd see how dependent on them we are. Some people just wanted the biggest party of their lives—the party Prince had promised in song years before. Everyone seemed to be expecting a big deal. As for me, I feared some loony business as a result of people's expectations and actions, and we lived in a big city, so I wanted to take my family out of town for a celebration. Yes, I thought, a camping kind of New Year's party—away from the city full of millennial doomsdayers.

The plan took shape pretty quickly. Katie, Richard, and I, along with our close family friend Joni, would take Caleb camping for New Year's weekend. Katie and I took a scouting trip east from San Diego to identify the possibilities. On our first night, we stayed at a big RV park in the Coachella Valley. It was a beautiful place with great desert landscaping and three or four big pools. And we were the youngest people in that RV camp—by about thirty years. They were nice folks, but most were over eighty years of age—probably not the right place for a family celebration. We drove by Salton Sea, a natural, Dead Sea–like phenomenon that had fascinated me as a child, but by 2000 something had gone awry. Dead fish littered the beaches, and the neighborhoods surrounding the lake stunk to high heaven. We drove on as I scoured a free camping magazine for options.

"What about this?" I read aloud: "De Anza Springs is one of the largest clothing-optional resorts in North America." I said it with my announcer voice, for comic effect because I couldn't imagine that Katie would want to go. She was not known for an adventurous streak, and while she'd been to clothing-optional women's festivals, those events were all-women. I couldn't imagine my lesbian lover of penis-free bodies consenting to even a night at such a place.

"Not a bad idea," she said with great nonchalance. I stared incredulously at her from the passenger seat.

"Really? You want to stop there tonight?" I interrupted myself: "Wait. Why do you want to stop there tonight?"

Though she was not known for being adventurous or for seeking male company—clothed or otherwise—she often offered an odd line of logic. It was the kind of logic you couldn't see coming, but it was sometimes reasonable. See, Katie is sensitive. That is, she can only stand cotton next to her skin. She wears cotton; she sleeps nude in cotton sheets. She's sensitive. And being naked in a temperate climate sounded, well, comfortable.

"Well, alrighty, then!" I declared, always interested in visiting a new alternative community. I'd been to nudist camps and events on a few occasions, but, as we drove, my enthusiasm increased. Yes! This was perfect.

"If this place is great, just think of it!" I gushed, as I started to put it all together. "It's the perfect place to avoid the New Year's kookies! They're sure to have some kind of party, and that'll feel like a celebration to Caleb. And even if there are kooky millennium people there, they'll be relatively harmless."

"How do you figure that?" Katie asked.

"No way to conceal a weapon!" I said triumphantly.

"Good point," she said, and on we drove.

Indeed, the place was perfect. Nice folks, nice facilities. We even decided during that first trip to store our RV there full-time and just drive out to use it when we wanted to. It was only an hour away from our home. It was perfect, and, truthfully, I'd never seen Katie so comfortable on any trip. Nothing was rubbing her the wrong way.

Immediately I turned to scheming about how to convince the rest of our family that this was a good idea.

The following weekend, I made French toast, and after breakfast I pulled out the stack of brochures I had picked up at De Anza. One was for De Anza, and then two or three more were for other nudist resorts around California. I figured a variety would help buoy my argument; plus, De Anza's brochure didn't actually depict naked people, mostly scenery. Some of the other brochures showed nudity, and, wow, the people just looked like happy families on vacation—only naked.

I started off by reminding Caleb that Katie and I had been on a really great trip away. I told him of the stinky Salton Sea and that we had found a wonderful place to park the RV when we weren't using it. And that was the place Katie and I thought we should all go for a New Year's celebration. "Look!" I said, "I brought some brochures."

He looked with interest as I showed pictures of the desert landscape, and I noted his approval of the two swimming pools. At that point I said, "Yes, the pools were great. And this place is pretty unique in that people who swim there swim without bathing suits, because it's nice to be in the water without anything on." He nodded slowly. It is nice to be in the water with nothing on.

"Everyone swims naked?" he asked.

"Yep. No one has to wear a bathing suit. Katie and I didn't either." I confirmed.

"Okay," he shrugged.

"And at places like this—because this isn't the only place where people don't have to wear bathing suits—people sometimes just walk around without any clothes on, because it's hot out, and it's nice not to have clothes on." I said this as casually as I could.

"*Everybody* walks around naked?" His eyes widened.

"No, not everyone." I saw his shoulders relax a bit. "But camps like this are called 'clothing optional resorts,' and that means that no one has to wear clothes, if they don't want to." He chuckled a bit; I could tell he was visualizing the display.

"They just all have their peckers hanging out. Ha!" He guffawed at the thought.

"Well, unless they have other things hanging out!" I laughed too. "See, look." I opened another brochure that showed a couple with a child, chatting, all in the nude. More nude people were playing volleyball in the background. (What is it about nudist volleyball?)

He laughed and pointed, then asked, "Do they have to be naked?" And I said, "No. Well, only for swimming." He had already accepted that part.

Caleb was already a live-an-let-live kind of guy. And if people wanted to be naked—and he didn't have to—well, that was okay with him. And here were some pictures—he was checking it out. I offered further explanation.

"It's a little weird at first, but then it just seems normal to see people walking around naked." I also reminded him that in our household, we had no particular modesty going to and from the shower. I reminded him that it was just like that—only with strangers.

"Does it look like a fun place?" I asked. He was nodding, with reasonable enthusiasm, until we opened one brochure that showed a family of four dining in the camp's restaurant. The family was sitting in a booth, on towels, all naked. The man and the woman were smiling. The son and the daughter were smiling. And I have to admit it looked something like the inside of a Denny's. A naked Denny's. A naked Denny's in 1984, to judge by the hairstyles. And as we turned the page, the social dissonance was just too much for my nine-year-old son.

"That's just nasty!" He shrieked. "But, but . . . why, why do they want to go in a restaurant *naked?*" He was sputtering and pointing at the photograph. "I'm not going in a restaurant with no clothes on! I'm not going to that kind of place!" He had been sitting, and he rose to his feet, horrified. "People are eating! Why do they want to do that?"

I must admit, I couldn't as easily explain why a family of four would want to sit in an orange and yellow plastic diner booth in the nude. I wasn't as outraged as Caleb, but I didn't really want to do that either. His live-and-live philosophy had worn dangerously thin with this revelation. I tried to laugh it off. It really was funny, but he wasn't ready for a good chuckle.

"No," he told me. "That's just nasty!"

"Okay, okay. Look, it's not any old restaurant. It's at the nudist camp. And you don't ever have to be naked at the restaurant. I wouldn't want to be either. But it's really nice to be naked outside by the pool." I quickly went back to the De Anza brochure. "See, this is the place where we'd be going—not that other one." I put away the silly naked diners. Phooey on naked diners. *Let's not look at that brochure any more,* I thought.

"I'm going to tell Dad and Joni about our New Year's trip too. Won't that be fun?"

"Ha-ha! Dad and Joni are going with us to the naked place!" He relaxed his outrage and found his funny bone again at the thought of all five of us wandering naked through the sagebrush. I could see the social voyeur in him come to life again. That's my boy.

Actually, they were easier to convince than I thought. I framed them as being no doubt more daring than Katie-the-non-adventurer, and I put forth my logic about no concealed weapons, and they were in. Richard also wanted a safe family activity for the weirdo-magnet millennium, and Joni couldn't believe that Katie had been happy at a camp full of naked mixed genders. "Really? She went there? And she wants to go back? Okay, this I gotta see."

We spent the last day of 1999 *en famille* and *au naturel*, splashing and playing in the pool. We all put our clothes on to go in and have burgers and pizza for lunch. And in the evening there was a family-friendly dance at the "Come as You Are Bar." Caleb and Richard played a game of pool, Katie and I danced, and Joni took up with some mustachioed character on the dance floor—then they snuck off for a hot tub. Caleb also found some kids his age to play with until they got tired and the kids curled up to nap on two sofas in the foyer. Richard sat with them until it was time to get up for the big countdown.

A person would be wrong to think that a nudist party would suffer from a lack of festive attire. People were fancied-up left and right. They just didn't have to be all the way covered up, that's all. I was fascinated to see that the party was far less sexualized than any party at a clothed bar might be. The women weren't strutting around with their breasts straining against spaghetti straps and spandex. They were just wearing sequins and rhinestones because they were pretty, and the bodies in their clothes were just bodies. They weren't being concealed as foreplay. We'd all seen each other naked already. Similarly, I didn't see men leering at women in the same way that often makes a person with children uncomfortable at a big party where adults are drinking. Everyone seemed to just be socializing—men and women talking with one another like people. And sure, there was still plenty of smooching and lewd innuendo at midnight, amid the noisemakers, right where it belongs.

I had been worried about the weirdos on New Year's Eve 1999, so we had headed for an encampment where the weirdos are all pretty normal. And I was right—no *chance* of a concealed weapon.

When I asked Caleb if he would go to a place like De Anza again, he said, "What? A naked place?" And I nodded. "Sure," he said. "What's the big deal?"

I nodded and shrugged, "Well, I don't know." Once a place is revealed as just being full of regular folks, there's no big deal at all.

19.

BUILDING THE GOOD BODY

My mother started losing her memory in her late seventies, and, for a time, she moved in with me. The odd thing about her memory loss is that she has begun talking to me as though I were the teenager she battled with—over many things—rather than as the adult she has known in the decades since. She says things to me like, "Oh, so I went to the store. I bought some of those Lean Cuisine meals. Those are low-cal. You can have those."

Forget that I gave up dieting and calorie counting decades ago in favor of living, moving, and loving. I have felt able to "have" any food I want for many years, and I wouldn't dream of choosing a Lean Cuisine meal (for so many reasons). Forget that. To her, I have a bad body against which she (and others) taught me to endlessly battle. And though I have forged a life of writing, speaking, teaching, witnessing, and helping others love their bodies, my mother is still trying to fix me. If she ever understood that my life had moved on past culturally normative body-desires, she has forgotten now. The construction and maintenance of the "bad body" is on my mind, especially as I politely decline the "slimming tea" she offers me each time she makes a cup for herself, complaining that her pants are tight and that her frail little body also requires revision.

This is how the "bad body" exists: we construct and maintain it through our social interactions. Outside of those interactions (and the way we replicate those messages and initiate those struggles within us), the body just *is*. Practicing yoga—or doing any physical exercise—can either be one more tool to create the bad body, or it can be a tool to create the good body. And the good body is a much more pleasurable place to live.

I started to discover my own good body as a personal home and a social location via movement, exercise, and yoga just after high school. I was a fat kid who grew into a fat teen (despite imposing severe food restrictions) and then a fat adult. Still, once freed from the high school gym class model of fitness, I loved a workout. Yoga practice was a particular refuge since folks are often focused on their own experience rather than looking at each other. Or at least they believe they *should* be focused within, so whatever body comparisons that are still occurring are not so regularly shared as they were in my Jazzercise classes, for instance. Something else was different about yoga than exercise class too. I noticed the calm buzz after savasana. A stop at the grocery after class left me wandering and smiling slightly at the produce. What was happening? I felt simultaneously aware of my feet walking through the aisles and calmer than usual about the outside world. The longer we can stay in the experience of the body, the less concern can arise about the appearance of the body.

We all live with powerful "bad body" scripts, and sometimes they're so common they become invisible. Many of us recite them to others without noticing it. Living in a colonized culture in which mind and body are separate means that we must constantly work to create and maintain the good body. Fortunately, mindfulness practices help refocus away from the good/bad dichotomy. Yoga practice can help too, as long as we remember that consumer yoga culture is created in the image of every consumer pursuit. It's a colonizing endeavor, driven by fear and desire for products—not practices—that purport to bring peace. And who is the colonizer? Any individual or business or organization or government who wants you to conform for reasons other than your own. A great deal of profit is made on the endless reform of bad bodies—sometimes even under the banner of yoga.

Even if we reject the "bad body" script, we were each socialized to carry it. Some are more heavily invested than others—and this investment is not based on appearance. That may be surprising to discover. As a fat, middle-aged woman with an occasionally visible disability, one might think that I should have greater anxiety about my "bad body" than a slender, able-bodied young woman, for instance. Because I spend time traveling, speaking, and storytelling on college campuses, I can report that appearance doesn't matter. What matters is the mindfulness to attend to the *experiences* of the body, rather than dwelling on the *appearance* of the body. That type of mindfulness is countercultural—it requires revision of the language used in pop culture about bodies (women's bodies most nefariously, but all bodies, surely). Any practice of yoga that prompts us to focus on the breath and positioning of the body during asana brings us right into an experience focus, rather than an appearance focus. That's good stuff. That focus can offer us experiences of real peace.

Think about your body. Do you have a good body or a bad one? If you have a socially laudable body type, you can probably recite its flaws anyway. That's polite social practice, after all, and maintains the idea that you've worked on that body and succeeded. You're maintaining the connection between virtue and body size, shape, and ability. You're "aging well." By living in these practices and language patterns, you're also maintaining the fear of failure. Your body could still fail to be a good body. That fear might cause you anxiety, or it might cause you to police other people's bodies along with your own. Subtle comments or glances project your fears onto others. This requires no ill intent on your part whatsoever. It's just how the social fabric is created.

Without me even describing the good body to you, you can envision it. The people in magazine ads have good bodies; most celebrities have good bodies; most politicians have good suit-bodies. It would be harder for them to get elected otherwise. Governor Christie of New Jersey is an anomaly who cannot take his body out of the conversation in elections. You know that—maybe even thought of him as soon as I mentioned politician-bodies. You know what a good body is. We all do.

A bad body is anything else—but particularly a fat body, an old body, or a disabled body, unless it's heroically disabled (think about the marathon-running amputee with the fancy metal feet). In North America and Europe, given our collective participation in historical (and current) trafficking of people from Africa and Asia, whiteness is also part of the "good body" trope. Conforming to a fairly rigid two-gender system is also imperative for the good body. You already know these things, but I'm reminding you because body-hierarchy socialization becomes invisible to us if we receive enough privilege to ignore it.

Look, it's not *my* opinion that you have a bad body; your culture has already defined that. But someone you care about or admire has reinforced that message. Maybe lots of times, through a variety of words and looks, as in the case with my mother. Perhaps there have only been a few comments about a funny nose or a pinchable bit on your waistline, but you carry them nonetheless. These bad body messages can even come from yoga or meditation teachers you admire, from whom you otherwise benefit. People are complex, and each one of us can offer input that validates bodies or input that supports the "bad body" trope. The latter usually happens unconsciously and requires gentle community for correction.

My yoga teacher (with whom I would eventually apprentice, as a teacher) was expert in offering modifications for various bodies. Indeed, people with injuries sought her out for rehabilitation. I was lucky to find her back in 1992. As yoga became more popular as a fitness activity, the people drawn to teaching were often the hard-body fitness types who used to teach aerobics before they got hooked on vinyasa. Not surprisingly, their body biases and aims for slenderness, muscled, fitness, and conformity came right along with them. The consumer culture and media that follow the fitness faithful turned their spotlight on yoga too, supporting and justifying pursuits such as attainment of the yoga butt or Breath of Fire abs.

Here's the cultural message none of us avoids receiving: if you have a good body, you're supposed to work to keep it. If you have a bad body, you're supposed to reform it. In truth, there's no wrong way to have a body, yet we each carry cultural scripts that place us in relationship to the "bad body." It's up to us to choose what to do with those scripts. Do we read from them faithfully, rewrite them, reject them, or partner with them in order to convert others to conform through self-deprecation, diet talk, and aging tragedies?

I have been fat all of my life. That was the first way I had a bad body, and then, as a teen, I developed an "overly sexual" body, according to my mother along with many men—strangers and known. Today I have an arthritic body, an aging body. I also have a queer body, though that isn't always visible. There are so many "bad body" messages. Maybe your gender and sex don't match up as some would like, or your skin color isn't respected or you're too tall or too short or not pretty enough, or you're deaf or disabled or your hair won't do what you'd like. Maybe you were told negative things, and you don't even believe them, except when you do, or when you're not vigilant enough, or when you get tired and just don't want to keep rewriting that cultural script every minute of every day.

Let me remind you that the "bad body" stories are not the only stories—and that the fastest way to create a good body is by telling different stories. The good body still has to be re-created every day through those stories, but they are far less time-consuming and more health-inducing than hating the bad body.

Tell a "good body" story, because those are true too. I have a vibrant body, a capable body, an ecstatic body, a wise body, a playful body. Despite the fact that I don't often see myself reflected in the yoga magazine stories, and certainly not in the ads, I have a yoga body. As a teacher, I am constantly complicating the visual narrative of the "bad body" just by showing up. I'm sorry that the lie of the bad body is not easily erased from our consciousness or our culture. And we can add to our culture's stories about bodies. As we begin to change our own stories, to see a variety of bodies with love, our experience shifts. As we begin to increase who is seen as beautiful, who is worthy of fame and praise, the cultural lie of the bad body shifts. Change is possible, even though those are really powerful scripts. Just as no one now worries over whether they have an inadequately or excessively sexy elbow, at some point, maybe, we won't worry over thighs or bellies or boobs or faces either. Today is not that day. And there are themes on which we can focus our stories to revive our bodies and minds, while acknowledging the context in which we live.

Pleasure. When I fear my body's decline, I punish it. I focus on stretching or exercising what I believe requires repair. "I used to have so much more flexibility in my shoulders," says the fearful mind. "I'd better make sure I work on those." And the body grumbles along arduously. When I focus on the pleasure in my body, the pleasure in sweating, refining a pose, breathing and moving, then fear diminishes. The body is then behaving capably, beautifully, and I am enjoying it. Fear dissipates with pleasure, and, paradoxically, strength and flexibility return. Not like when I was thirty, but as they exist today. Pleasure and contentment shift the narrative from fear.

Beauty. Take pleasure in a wide variety of bodies. Notice the way bodies move and differ, according to their own logic. So often we seek pleasure in conformity, in the repetitive appearance of certain types of faces, muscles, skin, or movement. Find beauty in a wide range of bodies you weren't taught were beautiful. When we expand how we see others, we expand how we accept ourselves.

Place and company. Notice when and where body judgments come up, and avoid those places and times. As numerous studies have shown, girls feel worse about themselves and their appearance after reading fashion magazines. Which metaphorical fashion magazines are you reading? Where do you go, and when do you feel your "bad body" most acutely? This is particularly important to notice in yoga classes, studios, and mindfulness communities. If you feel up to it, point out why you're withdrawing your participation. Offer resources. There's no guarantee your comments will be well received, but chances are that "bad body" community is unconscious and that revealing it could mean its improvement.

Language. Notice the kind of language you use with others and help your friends and loved ones if they are interested in uncovering their language biases too. I was grateful the time my friend pointed out to me that I had described my yoga teacher as being in her fifties but really beautiful. How had I said such a thing without even noticing? I meant she was both, and I actually used the word "but" without realizing I'd done so. Be brave enough to offer and accept help. Focusing on language choices may sometimes seem nitpicky, but we are wholly in control of our language choices. And these shifts add up.

Dignity. Remember that your dignity can heal others. Every time you calmly stand against the lie of the bad body, time stops. When someone sneers or laughs at your body and you calmly refuse to take the shame you are being handed, time stops. And in that brief quivering moment, a new world is born from your bravery.

The bad body was built to suffer. With practice and allies, we can move out of that "bad body" role every time we notice we're working that old script. We can also improve our yoga communities and our broader spheres of influence too. Yoga teachers especially have the power to create a class culture by what we omit, as well as what we allow. It's not as important to talk about the troubles with the "bad body" trope as it is to focus on embodied pleasure, contentment, and equanimity. Simply omit negative influences and gently redirect people's language when needed. Suffering can be soothed through solidarity. There are a lot of "bad bodies" out there. Yours is but one of them. And, sure, the colonizer sometimes tries to convince you that placing your body in hierarchy with others will soothe you. You may have a bad body, but it's better than someone else's. A keen awareness and great gentleness are needed to heal from this deception. And we can heal, one dignified moment, one partnership, one new story at a time.

20.

SELF-HELP, FITNESS, AND FEMINISM

Come to a comfortable seated position; use the blanket to elevate your hips so you can sit with the spine straight. Close the eyes and rest the hands gently in the lap.

So begins the yoga class. And just yesterday, as we sat quietly, receptively, in a meditative pose, the teacher said, "Everything in your life is the product of decisions you have made, ways of being you have chosen. If you want a different life, make different choices."

These words were offered as inspiration for our practice, as is often the case in yoga studios. The contemplation is meant to inspire and empower. Ostensibly, we should feel good about the choice we've made to take a yoga class and about the positive thinking we're doing now that we're here. The lights are low, our breathing is slow and we are consciously receptive.

But hang on.

Is the teacher's utterance even true?

And does it have anything to do with the millennia-old practice of hatha yoga? Or is yoga in a North American studio as culturally bound, socially situated, and gendered as any other activity in people's busy (and largely uncritical) everyday lives?

Leaving off the question of how this type of affirmation/inspiration fits into the history of hatha yoga, we should certainly discuss how it fits into the landscape of platitudes women and others consume and create—to the detriment of being able to organize for gender fairness and respect for body diversity.

Think for a moment about the teacher's statement. Everything in your life is most assuredly *not* the product of decisions you have made.

We each live one life as the subject of our own stories and another as the object of other people's stories. As the subject of our own stories we have the power to create positive messages and images of love and forgiveness within ourselves. We can heal and embrace all of the identities we inhabit regarding gender, race, body size, ability, beauty, social class, et cetera.

As the object of other people's judgment, we have far less individual control. We don't escape being born into cultural, political, and economic systems that give more privilege to some groups, less to others. Some identities are achieved; others are ascribed at birth. Most of us begin, at birth, experiencing either privilege or oppression based on certain identities, and these experiences influence us deeply. This must be acknowledged if we're to unlearn the internalized oppression most people carry as a result of simple things such as being female, transgender, or intersex, being people of color, disabled, queer, working-class, old, et cetera. You know how the list goes on. We each live two lives, related to our various social identities and stories. While it's possible to influence ourselves from within as the subject of our stories, influencing the way we're treated by others usually requires collective effort. It requires dialogue and sometimes unpleasant struggle. It requires the best kind of feminist action and an understanding of how oppressions intersect and how privilege becomes invisible.

And speaking of privilege, being truly present to how we're creating our lives requires us to question how some activities come to be "rich people mostly" or "slender people mostly" or "white people mostly" or "young people mostly." Especially activities like yoga, which are intended to be accessible to all. No one plans for exclusions. Yet they happen. Only certain people feel comfortable; only some have access. Exclusionary circumstances are changeable though not solely through personal decision-making.

So why is it so attractive to believe that all we have to do is change our minds, eat more kale, do more yoga, and life will be grand? Why do we pay people to tell us so—and in particular, since women far outnumber men as yoga practitioners—why do *women* want these messages?

It seems far easier to change oneself than to change oppressive systems, for starters. It's far more comfortable and familiar to take the blame for one's own semi-miserable, occasionally blissful conditions than to take responsibility for being part of a group that cooperates in its own subjugation. And it feels good to feel powerful.

I would never argue that people aren't powerful. This is why discernment and complexity are needed in the messages we create, purchase, and consume. We're simply far too obedient, sitting in a dark comfortable room feeling good about accepting what's being said to us.

Remember, there is no part of human culture that was not created by humans, and we have the power to change policies and politics. Cultural trends are generally a reflection of widely held beliefs. That's why we need to do the personal work of eradicating the sexism, racism, homophobia, and all of the interlocking oppressions within us. That's not so simple, and it requires real questioning and discussion, real peer support, and physical fortitude.

That's why yoga, meditation, and other fitness practices are great. So are critical thinking, kind questioning, and community organizing. Let's build those into every setting we inhabit, including our yoga studios. Let's thoughtfully engage a wide variety of messages we hear—from body shaming to victim blaming to culture-blindness. Non-feminist, racist, classist, and ablest environments will continue be the norm (invisibly for those who regularly inhabit them) if we don't transform them. And that's not just negative thinking.

21.

HOW THE WOMEN'S MOVEMENT RUINED EVERYTHING

I feel most like my mother when I am discontent, when I hold a griev-ance, especially against someone I feel entitled to punish, if briefly—a corporate representative, by phone, or perhaps a lover or child. I feel most like my mother when my past victimization can be rehearsed and turned into a story for retelling, one that triggers pain, pity, and con-sternation ad infinitum. I am my mother when I cause myself pain, as I see her causing herself pain again and again.

Do you tell your life stories as a series of things that happened to you, or as a series of things you did? Are you the subject of your stories, or are you the object of someone else's actions?

When my mother moved in with me in her seventy-ninth year, we became two of a kind, different only in that I am also the one who pushes away, creates distance, finds an escape route and uses it. Perhaps we all construct ourselves in relationship to our parents, choosing, with fervent irritation, how we will be different from them and only glimps-ing briefly how we are like them, sometimes despite our best efforts, sometimes with pride.

All of my life I have heard my mother's stories about my father's alcoholism, the difficulty of living with his dark, brooding times, his moodiness, his retreats, the way he spent the family's money on alcohol and then claimed he didn't, how much money she had saved before they married and how quickly it was all gone as a result of his addic-tions. He left when I was eight years old to become a one-weekend-a-month dad, and as I aged I heard other stories too. She actually asked me to lunch once when I was in my twenties to find out whether I thought my father was gay. Before I could answer, she recited a list I'd never heard that seemed to more than confirm her suspicions that he was sexually and romantically involved with both men and women during his life—and during their marriage. The clandestine meetings, the flirtatious friendships, the alliances with known homosexual men, the times she caught him, in compromising positions on two occasions, with men, at parties, and, of course, his penchant for piano bars. I listened in awe to her list and at its conclusion replied, "It seems like you answered your own question."

"Yes, but what do you *know*?" she asked, as though I might have been given a truth that she hadn't been. As though, being queer myself, I might have some special knowledge that didn't require being told something outright. Perhaps if you're gay, you can see a rainbow arcing off the other gays in bright sunlight. What did I *know*?

"I know that he's alluded to being like me but born in a different generation and that his declaration ended with telling me he was proud I'm an out lesbian," I said. I thought I understood what this had meant. I knew not to go further and felt he'd been clear enough in what he'd said. His statements were actually quite effusive. He had been drinking, as he often was when he initiated any conversation whatsoever with me, and then he had gone on and on. He told me about how he and I had a lot in common, things that might surprise me, and that he was raised in a different time and that things might be different for him today. He told me that he was proud of me for loving whom I chose and that he wanted me to know that he and I were very, very, very similar in many ways, but, well, it was a different time. I nodded as he carried on. As my mother stared at me through her furrowed brow, I recalled that one of my father's best friends, Bob, was out and gay. My father said he always respected how Bob didn't flaunt it. No one could tell just by looking at him.

When she moved in with me, my mother told these painful stories almost daily. She had begun to focus her storytelling on childhood a few years earlier, when I first noticed her memory slipping. I've read that it's common for older people to have more vivid memories of childhood, and she seemed so pleased with the ones about her father especially. But then, by the time she moved in with me, those seemed lost, and only the painful childhood stories remained. Perhaps because I resemble my father, seeing me daily seemed to invoke stories about him. Somehow she never spoke of my stepfather, the man who was abusive to me and ultimately prompted things to be said between my mother and me from which it was difficult to recover. I forced her choice between us at fourteen, and she chose to stay with him and let me go.

One day, tired of the repetitive stories of my father's alcoholism, I turned to her and said, "I understand that it was very difficult to live with him. I'm so sorry for your pain. And you're talking about things that happened more than forty years ago. Isn't there something nicer to recall?"

She stared and me and stammered, "Forty years? Well, no, was it? Forty years." And she didn't say more for a while.

Sometimes telling a difficult story is a way of getting some air around a topic—sharing a burden with friends—and sometimes it's a rehearsal for emotional pain, a way to arouse demons that could just as well be left sleeping. No one else can tell you the difference, but you can feel it, with a bit of discernment. It may be important to share a story during the period of seeking understanding, experiencing grief. And when the unburdening works, at some point, the story needs to be put down—only picked up again for someone else's benefit. No one benefits from these stories my mother tells, least of all her.

My mother was born during the Great Depression and became adult in a period of unprecedented economic growth in the United States. She tells beautiful, wistful stories about how people pulled together during World War II, planted victory gardens, hung flags in front of their homes, and commemorated those who died as heroes. The fight against evil felt good, and winning it felt even better. The end of the war brought a series of government programs aimed at creating a white middle class, and they did so brilliantly. Opportunities never felt like handouts in that era; they felt earned, perhaps in part because government decisions felt like the decisions of the people far more so than they do today.

She and her family were working class and white and used the privilege of those new social programs wisely. Of course, stories about privilege are hidden in stories about hard work. I remember both of my mother's parents as resourceful, hardworking people. My grandfather was a police officer and a carpenter, always building little things and inventing strategies to increase convenience. My grandmother was a secretary and homemaker who wrote notes and telephone messages in shorthand. I coveted her ability to read that strange language that was all her own in our household. They bought a house and prospered in the fifties in part because of their hard work and in part because they were given opportunities that many Americans were not. Funny how people don't know to appreciate the bounty of whiteness or being part of any group that gets a privilege that others don't have, but they know how to protect those privileges from interlopers when the time comes to do so. We are each capable of maintaining a sense of knowing and ignorance of what we know, the former dredged, by necessity, from the unconscious and concealed again as quickly as it emerged.

In current times too, we envy what we feel we don't have, even if the evidence shows we have greater access to what we want than others. Perhaps the prosperous 1950s bred envy in white women born to upwardly mobile families such as mine. Female beauty was already a competition with complex and dubious rewards, as it remains. We learn young that male attention can be both a prize and a punishment. We need male approval to be allowed to just get by in the world, to prosper, to be thought sensible, or to receive rewards. Perhaps envy of others' ease, others' gifts, the ways others have to work less or will receive more—perhaps this is not peculiar to women at all. We can all feel envy, but, when it comes to our children, fathers are not in direct competition with their sons in exactly the same way as women are with their daughters. Women age into ugliness or invisibility, often both, and their daughters can be a reminder of what they had (or could have had but didn't) and what they will never have again. Even mothers who love their daughters very much often see their own complex negotiations with beauty replayed and question their own and their daughters' judgments. Because navigating gender oppression is so seldom discussed and expectations change, each generation does it alone without enough help from mothers. Hindsight can bring clarity, forgiveness, or a feeling of foolishness regarding the decisions we had to navigate without help, without discussion, without a full awareness of what was at stake. Decisions about appearance and beauty and flirtation and sexuality are like that, and women often come to their daughters damaged, just as men do in their ability to relate to girls as people. Men mostly come to daughters as protectors or foes or not at all. What other social models are there? But those tragedies are comparatively simple. A lack is easier to manage than a chaos of missed and unspoken expectations, fears, and reprimands. As Rebecca Solnit writes, "For mothers, some mothers, my mother, daughters are division and sons are multiplication; the former reduce them, fracture them, take from them, the latter augment, enhance."

In that era of unprecedented economic growth after World War II, prosperity felt due, a prize for vanquishing evil in the war, a prize for the intelligence of the atomic age, a prize for the science fair miracles of the human ability to create abundance, push nature harder, and increase consumption in manifold ways as though that in itself were an accomplishment.

My mother was no calm conformist. She was brilliant at the tasks of modern women: maintaining propriety, beauty, and deference while giving her intelligence its due. She rose like a phoenix from Depression drudgery and became a pioneer in the new frontier of gender equity, a landscape in which female ingenuity could improve her chances for gain without disturbing the status quo of male superiority. In the 1950s, white middle- and upper-middle-class women became masters of manipulation without ever managing to run the household fully. They managed their men, making sure that they looked good at work and were cared for at home and in turn that they provided the foundation and ornamentation to make their wives proud of being adored and cared for.

This was the era of conformity and enjoyment, single women jockeying for the attention of men they could mold into providers, and married women maintaining the illusion of perfection in the family—adoration from husband and children, appreciation from their communities, and beauty, always beauty, as the glue that held the picture together.

My mother's parents sent her to modeling school at fourteen at the prompting of her older brother's new wife. Brother and wife had moved into the family home until they could get a place of their own, and the young bride took an interest in her grade-school sister-in-law, who seemed often self-parented with all adults working outside the home. My mother had no idea how the modeling courses would change her life. First, she felt her mother's pride in her—a scarce commodity—as she walked the runway during the modeling school graduation, primped and coiffed for public viewing and applause. Two hundred people turned out, in the grand salon of one of the city's fanciest hotels, and the next day at high school she was a celebrity. She and the other handful of newly minted models at her school walked the halls from then on as if they were on the runway, being seen to possess a knowledge that others lacked, the charm and grace of models, those most desirable of female attributes. They were not just seen as beautiful; they were respected for having broken the code. Prettiness one can be born with, but beauty is an alchemical invention, and the women who master the formula are special indeed.

My mother once told me that she hated the women's movement because during the early 1960s women would help each other. That was all over, in her view, when "women's lib" came along.

When she first said it, I puzzled and asked for an example. She turned a pensive eye down (another woman might have wrinkled her brow, but my mother had learned not to do such a thing to her face), and she paused. Then she said, "For instance, when I was trying to buy the modeling school where I worked as director, the owners didn't want to sell to a woman. I was the first single woman in the country to own a franchise and the only, for a long time to come. Still, the owners stood to profit greatly by the bet I suggested. I said they should see if I was ready for ownership by giving me a sales goal, and if I met it I could make the purchase. They set me a nearly impossible sales goal and thought only they would win, but if I made the goal in the time allotted, I'd have the option to buy the franchise with the money I'd saved. Do you know every woman in that office pulled together with me to make that goal? They were beside me working long hours and staying cheerful and keeping up morale, and when I did it, they were happy for me. Everyone was thrilled!"

Her joyful memory spread light across her face, and then it darkened. "The women's movement ended all of that. Suddenly it was every woman for herself. Everyone wanted to get something, and no one cared about working together like that anymore. There was competition, and the loss of camaraderie with other women was tragic. It's tragic what the women's movement did to end women working together."

I considered this story for a long time and still imagine its nuances, the way my mother's coworkers must have rejoiced in her victory, the way they must have felt uplifted by her ability to manipulate the men in charge and change the rules to suit her aims. I feel some pride in my mother's ingenuity in that story. The director of a business she longed to own, barred from purchasing it because of her sex, she crafted a clever path through thorny territory. She prevailed while remaining an ally to the men she beat. She gained their support and counsel over a period of years because she remained beautiful, allowed them to keep their status and glory, even as they lost the bet. She could win and still make them smile when she entered the room with a pretty face and an air of deference.

Suddenly there was competition rather than camaraderie, she said about the women's movement. Many others felt that feminism engendered sisterhood. Not her. She had become accustomed to being the bold, bright one with the moxie to challenge men and get all the girls in the office behind her. Suddenly everyone wanted what men had—the right to make decisions and determine their own destinies, open bank accounts, and make purchases without permission. Or if they didn't want those things, they thought they should. And beauty, women still wanted beauty and became all the more aware of what it could it buy. I think the women's movement ironically helped the business of modeling and charm schools to boom. So many more opportunities opened for women, yet the mass media was at work maligning the possibility of lost beauty and poise among feminists. The very word "feminist" quickly became an undesirable label, even as feminists were succeeding in creating positive social change for all genders. The doors were opening, yet women continued to be judged on looks. Modeling schools—with mottos like "be a model, or just look like one"—were big business. By the eighties, "personal development" became one of a series of "smart choices" women could make about their futures, and even corporations hired those schools to make sure the women they employed upheld a professional image. And too it seemed that every fourteen-year-old girl wanted to be in the magazines, and learning the rules of beauty was still the way to go. By then we knew we had to compete, and not just for a husband. One had to look beautiful for a job and continue looking beautiful for men who could leave and find a younger woman in an era of increasing acceptance for multiple divorces. For all the tales of women who "took men for everything in the divorce," the statistics don't bear out that cultural story. Divorce created and still creates poverty for women (because they are more likely to earn less and maintain care of children), so the ability to successfully manipulate personal appearance is a powerful skill.

I was born in the era of the "second wave" women's movement. But that parade never marched down the suburban street where I lived. The tragedy of how some women relate to their daughters—as a promise for fulfillment that turns to either disappointment or envy because, of course, no person can provide contentment to another—is both a response to experience and a lesson for the future. No wonder some mothers don't protect their daughters; no one protected them. Patriarchy is participatory. Daughters and mothers are set up to fail at the relationships that matter most to us. And in that generation of entitlement, the pain was both acute and absurd. We had so much more than before. But we didn't have each other's love. We never felt we had enough.

Did I get fat to remove myself from a beauty competition with my mother? I wanted her peace and happiness more than anything as a child. And she just didn't know how to be peaceful and happy. How did I know that I was more beautiful than she was? Somehow I knew that I *could* be, and though we play the scripts we're given in the cultural dramaturgy, we play them differently. If I made a decision to be fat, I made it before I was even aware of making decisions. I have been fat all my life. But I remember learning, as I learned to understand language, that it was not a good thing, that it invoked pity and disdain, and that my mother was both ashamed of my appearance and somehow happy that I was a project to be fixed rather than an object of envy.

Has daughter-love for aging mothers increased the number of fat women in this age of abundance and envy? Government programs are no longer about helping individual families to prosper, as in my mother's youth. We have all been left to personal ingenuity and social position. Public sentiment toward social programs such as those begun after World War II is that they would be tantamount to socialism today, even at the same time that we glorify that era as one of personal determination.

How do we return to consider the past, of a nation or of a childhood, with the insights and resources of adulthood? With practice, it's possible to imagine the self of today standing lovingly beside the childhood self to offer love and reassurance. Perhaps we can also become capable of projecting ourselves forward into the lives of the people we will become, people no longer troubled by these current circumstances and who have a whole new set of problems. They will have solved these current problems long ago. This could be a salvation, to look on time as a mutable part of the story, to let ourselves be exactly as we are in the pain of the moment, while also being as we will be, as we have become—capable of returning to the past to give that child a pat on the back, capable of coming to our current selves as a future person more wise and capable of perspective and calm analysis. More capable of love.

22.

HA-HA. YOU'RE SO FAT!
(ANATOMY OF A PUT-DOWN)

Recently at dinner, my neighbor's five-year-old grandson Taylor watched me sit down and said to his grandpa, at full volume, "Ha-ha, she's even fatter than me! She's *fat*." He finished with emphasis, looking at me out of the corner of his eye, because clearly those statements were for me too. Grandfather, along with two others at the dinner table, did that pullback, that sucking up of air and saying nothing, that we've all learned to do in awkward social moments.

I know this child—not well, but I've had meals with him before, seen him in the neighborhood. He's never called me fat before, but who knows? Maybe he was bored and looking for a bit of entertainment. He seemed to want to amuse himself with adult discomfort or perhaps just with my shame.

Though he was talking to his grandfather, trying to find an accomplice in the joke, I said, "Hey, Taylor, did you just call me fat?" And he turned to me, with a little bit of fear on his face because, whoa, this isn't how it's supposed to go. I was also speaking at full volume, for the other diners to hear. "I don't think there's anything wrong with being called fat, because it's not bad to be fat. But you know what? Some people think that's an insult word, so maybe you shouldn't go calling someone fat. Better wait until you hear people call themselves fat. Then you know they're okay with it, and then you can use that word too. Otherwise, you might hurt someone's feelings. You're not hurting my feelings, though. Fat is just one of the ways bodies can be. So what?"

His mouth hung open for a moment, staring at me. One of the other diners, relieved, said, "Wow, that was a really good answer."

I nodded and added, speaking to her (but also so that young Taylor could hear), "Well, some people have learned that being fat is shameful. That's why everyone goes silent when a kid says something like that. It's good to show them that there's no shame needed."

Grandfather raised his eyebrows, impressed, then turned to Taylor and said, a bit tauntingly, "She got no shame for you!" Taylor's mouth still hung open. "You want to know what shame is?" he continued. "That's when you're caught stealing something at the store and everyone sees you get caught. That's when you feel shame."

I'm not sure what Taylor was absorbing at that point. He may've been thinking, *Wow, sometimes you pipe up and everything takes a hard right turn!* That's for sure, kid.

Kids learn from reflection and from trial and error just like adults. There's certainly no fast track, though. A little while later, he called his grandfather "old man" in a pointed tone meant to hurt. I gave him the *I see you* eyes after he said it, but I didn't speak.

I knew Taylor to be very smart and mouthy and forever fidgety at a dinner table. My grandson and Taylor are the same age. Though my first reflex might be to feel smug for how much better behaved he is than Taylor and how his parents definitely taught him not to feel or throw body shame, it's not like he's perfect. He could also poke a friend and say of someone else sitting at the same table, "He's fat!" (or "stupid" or "has slits for eyes" or "has stinky feet" or "eats salt for dinner"—or, or, or). Sure, he could, at five. And everyone learns that it's possible to elevate oneself by putting someone else down in a clever way. And if he learns that others will collude with put-downs and that he can feel a sense of belonging by creating an inside joke about someone else, it's not just possible. It's likely.

Furthermore, he could do that at school and never admit to being that kind of person at the dinner table with his parents who don't approve of body shaming.

When my son was five, I overheard him with some neighborhood friends as they played a game on our patio. They were talking about *Teenage Mutant Ninja Turtles*. It was the biggest show on TV at the time. They were reminiscing about their favorite episodes, and my son chimed in with his favorite episode too. Blow-by-blow.

One thing puzzled me. We didn't have a TV. I asked him later where he'd seen that show, and he shrugged and said he'd never seen it. When I told him what I'd overheard, he looked at me, sweet-faced as ever and said, "Oh, when I heard other kids talking about the show, I memorized what they said so I could tell the story again the next time kids were talking about it. Everyone talks about it. I want to talk about it too."

I nodded. That made sense.

The woman seated next to me at the dinner table when Taylor commented on me being fat—one of the people who recoiled in silent horror when he said it—is a kindergarten teacher. She's also the one who said I gave a really good answer. After Taylor turned his attention elsewhere, she told me that she has seen children in her class say this sort of thing, trying to make another child feel bad. She said she never knew what to say.

Really?, I thought. Even though a person has children or works with children, somehow one may never find an adequate response. And maybe that means we aren't really looking for one.

Kids learn that there's power in befuddling adults. Just like there's power to be gained in successfully hurting another person's feelings. It's a sad kind of power, but it's power nonetheless. Taylor was definitely puffed up in that small moment when everyone fell uncomfortably silent before I spoke.

I'm also thinking about the wording in Taylor's specific comment. "She's even fatter than me." He's not a fat child at all, though I've seen him put away some dessert—four brownies that very night—so I imagine people have threatened him with becoming fat. "Quit eating those, or you'll get fat." That's the sort of thing people tell kids all the time.

Still, this is a sophisticated game Taylor had already learned to play well before his sixth birthday. Not only is he controlling adult behavior, albeit briefly, and not only is he bonding with someone over the put-down of another, and not only does he know which things to say to shame a grown woman, he knows how to ameliorate his own image in the process.

While most adults put aside direct put-downs in favor of subtler *shade*, many adults still think that if they put themselves down too, they're not really being meanies to include others in the insult. It's one of the ways that fat people themselves can perpetuate fat hatred at the same time that they seek community. "C'mon," that kind of inclusionary insult says. "We're all big and gross. I'll admit it before you throw it in my face—and pull you in while I'm at it."

My mother still uses the kind of insult Taylor used, regarding food. She's not fat either. Recently we were eating oatmeal and after spooning brown sugar into her own steaming bowl, she looked over and compared it to the color of my oatmeal. She said, "Wow, I put more sugar in my cereal than everyone . . . except you."

We were the only two people at the table. I took a deep breath and replied simply, "I didn't put any sugar in mine. It's dark chocolate."

She sat upright in surprise, and without missing her volley, replied. "Oh! Well, if you want to have *chocolate* for breakfast, I suppose that makes sense." No one could call her a bully. No sirree.

That Taylor's a smart kid. I'll bet you know some like him.

One of the best things about parenting (and grandparenting) is the constant opportunity to up our own game. And we get to choose which game it is, and what we're teaching. Whenever there's a silence after an insult like Taylor's or about any unspoken bias—like when a kid innocently comments on someone's race or social class—we can pay attention. Make a mental note. And then, talk that stuff through with peers so that we invent the answers that teach something positive the next time. We rarely have the perfect comeback when we're surprised. But why be surprised by things that are said or intimated again and again? I'm certainly not surprised when someone speaks ill of fat. It happens all the time; Taylor's comment, at least, was clear and direct.

Teachers should plan ahead for touchy topics too. And if you think that's not their business—stick to the lesson plan—think again. If we want kids to learn math, they'll focus better if they don't feel shamed (or like they need to plan their next attack).

That's all I did when I spoke up. I had invented a better answer, and I delivered it with clear, calm eye contact. Everyone at the table felt relief, and hopefully Taylor learned something. At the very least, he added a new response to the possible repertoire of answers adults can give.

Beginning in childhood, I was handed the same shame every fat person has been handed. And for the first part of my life, I carried it. Then I learned to put it down. And then I learned to talk about it. You can too. If we want kids to grow up and take responsibility for their words and actions, then it's time adults do it more ourselves.

23.

PASSING IT ON

My mother-in-law already thought I was too fat and didn't mind telling me so. She said being fat and pregnant was going to harm the baby. She commented on how much fatter I was getting as the baby grew. I gained eighty pounds during that pregnancy, so she was right. Of course, when the baby was born healthy at nine pounds four ounces, she claimed her own genetic material had saved him from the harm I'd done as a fat vegetarian. This made me an incomprehensible oxymoron, of course—fat and vegetarian—but no need to revise her ideas. She remained sure of everything. She was also interested in the conformity of my feminine appearance. When she visited the hospital room during my active labor, she said to her son, "Couldn't she put on a little make-up?"

I shrieked from the bed, "Get her out of here!" She and the rest of the family had the good sense to go out to dinner while the baby was being born.

Contrast her views to the response my body received from local women during a visit to the Bahamas when I was eight months pregnant. I was indeed large, but the meaning of size was significantly different. For the women who saw me (it was always women who commented), my size meant health. I was going to deliver well and the baby would be healthy. A big round pregnant woman was a blessing in motion, and women ran out of shops to put their hands on my belly and exclaim, again and again, with smiling faces, "You're *enor*mous!" Sometimes they'd add, "What a big healthy baby you're going to have." And then they'd joke with each other and me, saying, "No, she's not having one baby. That's twins!" "Definitely triplets!" "Still a month to go? More than one baby in there for sure!"

At first overwhelmed by the attention and unexpected touching, I quickly settled into the happiness my round body evoked. People smiled at my husband and congratulated him too, as though my roundness was proof of his good fortune and prowess.

Truly, even in the United States most people treated me more like a pregnant woman than like a fat woman during that time. It was a welcome relief from being generally seen as lazy and overindulgent. Being pregnant is at least creative; there is labor involved and a tangible outcome that is generally thought to be a blessing, so long as one is white, straight, cis-gendered, non-disabled, and not poor. This is how my culture understands the productivity of the fat female body. As my white breasts swelled with milk and I carried the new progeny in my fat arms, I was perceived as a fecund part of expansionist America, whereas poorer, browner Americans might be seen as a burden on the nation's brilliance.

He told me years later.

In middle school he began throwing away the cards and checks his paternal grandparents sent him at birthdays and Christmas. During college, my son considered changing his last name so that he'd have less connection to them. In addition to being racist, his paternal grandmother in particular just wasn't very nice. My son grew up listening to his father's stories of trying to please her, of her drinking. He had also heard the aforementioned story of her demanding I put on a more pleasing face during childbirth. That's a dramatic story, but I believe there was less gravity in my telling since she wasn't *my* mother. She was his grandmother, though, and he felt pain about her cruelty and judgments.

She once told him—when he was about six—that I was going to die an early death because I was too fat. He cried as he told me, and I can imagine how she must have spit the word "fat," because I'd heard her do it myself. She was a petite woman, still able to get in my face and look down her nose at me though she stood a good eight inches shorter. She belittled family members directly, no polite talk and withering glances—like my mother offered—about how things "should" be and how I just didn't measure up.

Joining a new family through marriage is about learning new ways. I remember once using my husband's check at a department store to make a purchase and having the cosmetics counter clerk look at me with recognition based on the name. My mother-in-law shopped there often and had spoken of me, apparently. The clerk said, "Well, you're just as pretty as she said you were. And she brags about how smart you are too!"

My mouth hung open, unable to believe we were speaking of the same person. The clerk repeated her name twice, my husband's name, and my name before I closed my mouth, nodded, smiled, and said, "Well, isn't that nice to hear."

That's how abuse-centered families do it sometimes, I learned. Close the ranks to protect from the outside; inside, it's brutal.

My son was raised differently, and he wasn't having it. She was a big meanie, and he refused to visit them anymore. He kept a relationship open with my mother. My mother is also a white racist, sweet as pie, opinionated, and funny, and I noticed how the barbs she threw about bodies slid right off of him. He was Teflon where I was fur, matted bloody through time from the injury of those comments, so everything stuck. One night when he was about ten, the three of us played cards while he ate from a box of movie candy in his shirt pocket—the kind of hard sugary bits that would make my mouth ache. He loved those things, munching as we played. She interjected occasionally, "Ew! I just can't stand to see you eat all that candy." "Caleb, it's making me sick. It's going to make you sick too." "You don't want to get fat on all that candy, do you?" "What can I do to get you to stop eating that candy?" She wrung her hands and gave him the same looks that had taught me hot shame and defiant determination as a child.

He just chuckled, unmoved by her remarks. His mind on the game, he'd chirp cheerfully, "I feel fine." "I'm not fat, grandma." "Candy's good."

It was all I could do to stay in my chair. I wanted to stand and scream at my mother, "Look at me! Why do you think that kind of shaming works?"

I felt both triumphant for holding my tongue and a coward for not speaking up on his behalf. He clearly didn't need it, though. She had long since stopped looking at my body, lost cause that I was. His was still a soul worth saving.

While I was pregnant, I developed a small jiggly pocket of fat that hung from the bottom of my baby-belly. It's still there now, decades later. I had been a certain kind of fat before the pregnancy. Distribution of weight matters. At 5'9" and about 220, doing six to eight aerobics classes per week, walking often, I was tall, strong, and shaped like a bombshell from another era. Still "too fat," but the kind of too fat that could be overlooked if a person liked a little extra potato and gravy with that plate of pork chops. I recall once, in Lamaze class, the men and the women being separated to make lists of the pros and cons of the pregnant body. I overheard men commenting on how hot their wives were now that they were getting some soft curves, bigger boobs. My husband commented, "Yeah, she already had great boobs and curves. Now it's getting a little out of hand."

Though I never stopped exercising, those eighty pounds I added during the pregnancy mostly stuck around after the birth. My youthful history with food deprivation played back after I stopped nursing and tried to lose some weight. Depression set in during my son's second year, something fierce. I'm sure that experience was part biological, part cultural. I worked too much; we struggled financially. I think my husband and I both felt trapped. That old feeling of not being worthy of food played back. And for me that feeling is chased by a righteous rage that yes, indeed, fuck you, I will live. The internal conflict became unbearable, and at twenty-five, before my son was four, I made a serious commitment to love myself as is and never diet again. I made a commitment not to eradicate myself through deprivation. Though I have my moments of feeling virtue in hunger, I have never dieted again.

That's already weird—having a mom who doesn't diet. That's how my son grew up.

He told me that when he was small, he didn't even know I was fat. I weighed between 280 and 315 pounds during that time. To him, being fat meant having a big belly, and I didn't have one, so he just didn't notice that I was . . . different. And I was active. I was his mom, likely invisible in familiarity. When he commented on this recently, he wondered aloud whether families who tend to be fatter ever speak to their children about the effects of fat stigma in the same way that Black families might speak to their children about being safe around the police in a racist culture, for instance. Sure, a fat kid can be an anomaly in a family, but not always. I pondered this and said no, I didn't think those conversations were common, primarily because a dieting mom is the American norm. Fat stigma is so internalized, an entire family of fatties being radicalized in that way would be unlikely. Sad thought. I hope it's changing.

This is what my son remembers: other people—his father in particular—warning him about his genetic propensity to become fat like his mother. To them, that meant he simply had to work harder and guard against a dangerous possibility. That's how he learned I was a bad sort of different, as a middle-schooler, from other people wanting to police *his* body.

Because I gave up dieting in favor of an "eat what I crave, when I'm hungry, and until I'm full" philosophy when my son was so young, he never knew a dieting mother. And while my commitment to eating, shame-free, in full view of others was shocking to some, my son reported trusting it. "Sure," he said, "people saw you eat cake and cookies and sometimes said they worried about your health, but what they didn't see was Dad's diet-and-binge ways of relating to ice cream, for instance. Dad stayed fit-looking, so no one ever knew his actual relationship to food. I think I got some of those habits from him. From you, I saw more balance."

Now in his late twenties, he notices that most people seem afraid to have sugary or fat-filled foods around—like they have to eat them all because they can't stand for them to just *be* there. When he brings a box of donuts to work, everyone acts like they hate him, even though they eat the donuts. This is the cultural norm. "Junk food" is both sinful and desirable. People's relationship with the food is obsessive. In those real-time moments of obsession, the focus isn't even on getting fat; it's on consumption. The food itself needs to be managed. Eat the donuts. Ignore the donuts. Rearrange the donuts in the box after taking half of one. This disordered relationship with food is related to fear of fat, but it is also separable in real time.

I'm glad he experienced more balance from me—and I still have those feelings of obsession too. Because I was a fat kid who turned into a fat adult, I don't always feel worthy of eating—anything. That's a tough thing to discuss, especially when it's happening. I'm not sure I *ever* discussed it with him. He didn't know the younger me who could keep from eating for weeks at a time, who would pass out from hunger and thirst rather than succumb to human needs. He didn't know the slightly older younger me who angrily rebelled against a culture that wanted me to disappear because I had a fat body. That character in me screamed, "Watch me eat cake, fuckers! Watch me lick the frosting from my fingers and reach for a second slice if I want to. Oh, yeah, you know you want to watch!" In a culture that has conflated sin with both sex and dessert, I was defiant in both landscapes. "You know you want it! Sex! Cake! You want to be me, and you want to be this cake I'm eating." My consumption became performative, and, interestingly, made me trustworthy to my son. "What you see is what you get" characterized this relationship. Sometimes excess, sometimes prudence, but an honest relationship, unhinged from social shame. As much as I could muster.

Women suffer from both the conflation of food and desire and the conflation of sex and desire. Food and sex are the two ways that we are meant to remain virtuous, nice, pure, abstinent. These messages are everywhere in our culture. It's strange terrain for a child to navigate with a mother, and it's where I lived—especially when he was little.

I've always known—even in moments when I eat more than my body wants—that choosing to eat is the healthier response to difficult feelings than choosing not to eat. Choosing sexuality is a healthier response to internal pain and external disdain than shutting down sensual desire. When I can't find balance—even still, decades later—eating is better than not eating. I don't encourage that paradox-ically virtue-filled death-wish feeling that comes with deprivation. I want to live.

I forget sometimes that my son has not known me all my life.

When my grandson was two, he and his parents visited me in Hawaii. We spent much of that visit in our bathing suits, in and out of the water. The baby was still in a diaper with no need for other clothes in a climate where the air caresses the skin. On the first day of that visit, my son's partner innocently posted a family picture of us on Facebook, and, of course, she tagged me. I started that Facebook page primarily to communicate with the people who read my essays and attend my per-formances and lectures. Since then, I've come to enjoy staying in touch with many of the people I meet in my travels. Still, I have thousands of "friends" I don't even know.

There had never been a picture of me in a bathing suit that was so available to so many people. If I were younger—part of the selfie generation—I could well be a selfie-fatkini activist, but I'm not. I write and speak about weight stigma, about bodies in culture, about the value of creating new cultural patterns. Why did I ask her to take the picture down? It took a few hours to handle my initial freak-out, and then I asked her instead to "untag" me rather than remove such a nice photo entirely. I felt embarrassed by my request. I was shocked that my snap reaction to being seen in a normal, terribly joyful family moment was to hide my body.

That's the power of cultural conditioning. And mostly I'm gentle with myself. I don't always choose the challenging route. If I'm tired or feeling vulnerable, I don't put my body on display unnecessarily. I don't always have to fight the good fight. But when it comes to my kids, I feel a failure if I don't. I want to be a positive part of what my grandson learns about bodies.

As a parent, my son will pass on messages about the body, about stigma, about size, and about food to his own son—both by example and with his words. If I were parenting my eighth-grade son now, I'd probably be capable of having those talks with him that he fantasizes fat families could have—to prepare their children for social norms and values about fat bodies—to mitigate the harm of fat stigma. He was chubby then, and kids teased him for having man-boobs. Soon he added a foot in height and became slender once more. He recalls being comforted by another family member's simple comment that his boy-fat phase seemed to be ending. He understood that he was not uniquely failing at having the "right" body. He was maturing normally through "a phase."

I didn't talk about his body, because he looked fine to me. I was the fat one. I wanted to shield him from comments like the ones his grand-mother made about me. I didn't want him to fear my death. I didn't yet know that some family members assumed him to be also defective because of my "bad genes" and presumed bad habits.

I hope I've passed along more than my genetic propensities regarding fat. At different times in my life, I've had different language with which to discuss fat. It was enough, in my early twenties, to give up dieting and become stalwart about my own worth and survival. A lot can be conveyed to children without words. And what he passes on to his son will be complex. His lessons may also include the kind of stories I couldn't tell. He might actually say words that explore per-sonal pain and social stigma, how they interact with health and kind-ness and worth.

My son might even be able to ask his own child questions I didn't think to ask him. Things like, "How do you feel about your own body, and how others view it?" As he grew, we spoke openly about racism and social class, gender identity, and ability. I stopped short of talking about fat stigma with him—even though I wrote about it for adult audiences. I hope that he'll do better at connecting the tough questions about his own body with the tough questions about other people's bodies. He already has a more complex schema for talking and listening and mak-ing meaning to offer his own son than I had to offer him.

He will do his flawed best, along with his partner, who has her own familial context with which to grapple regarding fat and body stigma. I will continue to do my flawed best as well. I'm still better at handling tough topics in writing, in planned interactions, than in off-the-cuff moments when my body feels revealed.

Parenting possibilities continue to unfold; I'm not dead yet. I will continue to do my part with my grandchildren and perhaps great-grandchildren. My nasty old body-policing mother-in-law was wrong, I hope, about my early death.

I'm definitely a different grandmother than my son had. Both in body and mind, I'm different. I'll continue offering the live performance of my body—the performance of dignity in difference—and I'm already relaxing more about photographs too. I'll continue to show evidence of self-love, along with passing on clear messages about self-love when I can. So will my son and his partner. My grandson's body will bear this understanding and I hope less social stigma as a result of our efforts.

24.

LEARNING TO FISH

Sometimes, as I tell stories about beauty hierarchy and appearance privilege, I meet people who want to claim that I'm focusing on petty interpretations. Not everyone thinks that beauty is so important. Just because some vain women want to have facelifts and breast augmentation doesn't mean beauty obsession is part of the cultural fabric that influences us all. Just because some men want trophy wives and wouldn't want to date a fat woman doesn't mean somehow the whole culture is influenced by their preferences. People also love stories about overcoming adversity and believe individuals should be valued for their talent and verve and hard work and beautiful hearts—not just their good looks. The best stories, after all, are about the triumph of the human spirit.

Sure. We love those stories. And we've also conflated beauty with virtue and triumph. Humans can hold multiple and conflicting views, ideas, and objectives. What looks right and seems right is influenced by fear and painful interpretations as much as by hope and gratitude—maybe more. We deny what we know in moments when those truths don't serve us or when they challenge us or pain us too much.

For instance, the same people who adore a story about true love based on interests and commonalities and connection would talk mad trash if George Clooney were to marry Melissa McCarthy. They wouldn't be saying, "Ooh, look at that gorgeous dress; I wonder if she's going to learn to speak Italian when she stays at the villa on Lake Como." No. They'd talk about why he chose to be with a fat woman. Forget that George and Melissa are in the same line of work, have much in common, and she's obviously smart and talented, just like him. They'd freak out because she's fat. And even though everyone knows this is true, it's still compelling to act like it's not when there's no specific example being offered. If Melissa and George announced the news, there'd be no talk about why she chose him, because theoretically every woman would choose him. He's been deemed influential (*Time* magazine), sexy (*People*), and talented (Golden Globes galore). He's been approved. I mean, she's great too. But appearance is what matters—especially for a woman.

My mother rented her home to a man and woman who recently married and are building a house nearby. She met the new husband first and then, a few weeks later, she met the wife. And she said that her opinion of the man changed for the better after meeting the wife. The bride was beautiful and had a lovely fashion sense, but as soon as she stood and walked, my mother reported, "She had a club foot! Can you believe that? Here's a handsome guy, successful in business, and, well, she's beautiful! But there she was," and then my mother aped her unsteady gait in a most unattractive manner.

For my mother, this was not an unkind story about the woman. It was a surprisingly lovely story about an impressive man who, somehow, against all odds, was able to heroically accept a giant flaw in his wife's appearance. Without knowing a thing about him, my mother imagined him to have those high ethics I described above—able to see his wife's inner beauty (or at least focus on her foxy face and slender body). This was also a story about the good fortune of a woman who was probably raised, fittingly, to expect less. In my mother's story, this woman should be grateful to have found such a saint.

We all manage social and cognitive dissonance. We can look at the facts of a situation and sometimes even discuss a topic intelligently and then turn right around and act the opposite of what we've just asserted is right. It takes effort to deny our socialization in favor of new knowledge. In fact, most of us were raised specifically to see the truth of inherent human dignity and deny it in the same instant. It's not new information that people are more than their appearance. We learn it in our most significant interactions with family, friends, and loved ones.

And still we'll forge ahead and put others in their places according to an appearance hierarchy that accords negative traits to unpopular appearance—whether related to gender, race, size, ability, age, or otherwise; appearance matters. We put ourselves in place in that hierarchy too. Unless she's chosen to live and think of herself differently, the woman with the unusual gait may indeed feel extra-lucky to have found a guy who doesn't mind her disability.

My friend asked my opinion recently about a child she saw in a department store dressing room trying on bathing suits. A fat child. Trying on a bathing suit that was tight and sparkly, not terribly modest. My friend made it clear, with her hand gestures, that she could see the child's flesh on the sides of the suit. The fat wasn't as fully covered as possible. And my friend wondered whether the adult accompanying the child had done her a disservice by giving in to the child's enthusiasm to buy the swimsuit. "I mean, that child will experience ridicule!" said my friend. "And she should know that she can't go dancing around looking like that in a public place, acting like she can expect to be treated like other kids." And let me insert here that my friend is both slender and African American. I asked her how old this child was. "About ten," she replied. I asked if she thought an African American child of ten would already know that our culture finds her "less than" because of race.

"Of course." She replied, thoughtful.

And so would it be helpful to tell that ten-year-old African American child to settle down if she were excited, dancing around her fabulous science fair project, because realistically she won't have as much privilege when it comes to learning about science, especially if she attends a public school in an impoverished area? Or would you not do that now, because most have come to accept that things like race and gender bias should be different, even though they aren't quite? But would that have happened fifty years ago? That a black child would be discouraged from unlikely professions and pursuits in order to save her feelings (or possibly even her life if she were to be truly shunned)?

My friend agreed partially yet still didn't think it was the same thing. And it's not the same thing. It's a related thing. What purpose is there in a loved one enforcing a negative message the child can't help but already understand? We make a pact with one another to ensure that children know the culture and how it will treat them. More useful would be letting them know how to preserve their dignity in a world that will warp their desires and values to suit the status quo. To do that, adults would also have to learn to preserve their own dignity too—or at least get started on that path. Most useful, perhaps, would be to show our children how we will stand with them to change cultural norms that devalue them, no matter the criteria.

It's too easy to think that people being judged can change if they want to. Fat people can lose weight. (We still manage to hold the view that fat people can lose weight, though 95 percent of diets fail, and we know people have different body types.) The boorish and unfashionable can learn to change their ways. Disabled people can do everything possible to appear "normal." And to a certain extent, it worked, when Claude Steele learn to whistle Vivaldi in public in order to put his Ivy League colleagues at ease about his blackness. Steele knew he was a threatening anomaly, as he writes in *Whistling Vivaldi: How Stereotypes Affect Us and What We Can Do*, so he developed strategies to mitigate the effects of social stigma. (His analysis is far more interesting and complex than my brief allusion to it here.) We all do some form of this, rather than doing what we could to collectively change social expectations. It's called identity management.

I'm an optimist. Naively optimistic, some would say, because I am indeed suggesting that large-scale social change can be initiated, by individuals, on a daily basis. We could start by acknowledging the cognitive dissonance of knowing that we will be judged poorly for being too fat or not attractive enough or letting our hair go grey, yet still espousing the view that "anyone can let their wonderful talent shine!" We can start by acknowledging and discussing the fact that certain messages and company sap our energy and cause feelings of low self-worth while other messages elevate us. We could do that without the weird caveat about how the "real world" is brutal and doesn't operate that way. Who on earth do we think is creating the "real world?" Real people, who also manage anxieties, seek privilege, and try to minimize the unpopular aspects of their identities too.

I've often been asked how I can be interested in sociology—it's so depressing. Others say, "Why do you want to focus on identity all the time? If you tell people they're being held back by the very systems in which they live, they'll just feel defeated. If you don't talk about it, then people will just proceed as individuals." That's what we should all be, they say, individuals, not identities.

Identity matters because social privileges follow appearance and story in a big way. And, paradoxically, appearance and identity are no big deal. Two people who find themselves goofy in love are no different if they're ugly or beautiful, old or young, gay or straight or otherwise. External forces may indeed burden them differently, but the core experience of being really hot for someone is pretty relatable. Humans are gorgeously complex. Like the little girl in the bathing suit, we already understand the game. And often we manage joy despite it. We know from the time we're children where we stand, and then we decide what to do about it. For me, connecting personal stories and social patterns is empowering because it reminds us that we are literally creating the world, even as it creates us. There is no part of human culture that wasn't created by humans. Sure, we are each born of the previous generations' biases and cruelty and unfair systems. We are also born of their hope, grace, and dignity. And through awareness, personal sovereignty, vibrant storytelling, and effort, we can awaken from previous generations' nightmares of injustice. Of course, we can. Social change moves slowly; it moves quickly; it doubles back. All of it happens because of people's stories. Multiple stories. There's no such thing as a "universal story."

There are, however, relatable stories. I've been writing and performing them for decades; audiences tell me how they relate. The body is the significant artifact in my stories and in your stories too. "Have a look at me and pull up all the judgments you can muster," I tell my audiences. "You don't even have to try, do you? It happened as soon as you saw me. You assessed many of the ways that I carry stigma and many of the ways I can wrangle privilege, based on what you saw. We each relate to the world based on our experiences and appearances and the ways in which we choose to show ourselves—even though some stories have been elevated, honored and others are barred, or at least discouraged, from being told. Diverse experiences add to human knowledge and perhaps compassion too." Our specificities are critical and magnificent.

Give a man a fish, it is said, and he'll eat for a day. Teach him to fish, and he'll never go hungry. The same thinking may apply to the creation of cultural stories. I can take your existing story and replace it with a better one, and you can have a better life. That's what happened with Eve Ensler's *The Vagina Monologues*. Ensler wrote a play that engaged people because it took a simple story—the vagina is bad, icky, and shouldn't be discussed—and changed it. Through the voices in her script, the story was transformed: the vagina is good and not disgusting and can be discussed just like any other thing of importance. That's a great reframing, and people were ready for it, and the play became a cultural phenomenon.

That show is teaching people to fish, just like many of the story-telling performances I've done to help people disrupt the tradition of body-shaming. I can disrupt that story and show you lots ways that people organize their lives outside of body tyranny, how the body can be a respected source of wisdom, and a great place to live. If your story hurts—and many stories hurt us—I'm happy to help replace it with one that serves you better. If enough of us live better stories, we even begin to shift the way social networks, social systems, and institutions impose rules upon us and how commerce keeps us buying. We can do all of that with better stories.

And my goal as a storyteller is bigger still.

I hope to tell the kind of stories that show you that stories can change, and that help us each develop tolerance for ambiguity and complexity. We are not limited to putting down one story to replace it with another—though sometimes healing is that simple. We can create stories and share them, and then later we can change our minds. We can learn from the body, from nature, from each other, from patterns wherever we see them, from intoxication, from silence, from sacrifice, and from pleasure. We can change as often as needed and this re-storying doesn't mean that we are adrift in a social sea, rudderless. It means that we create sturdier vessels, capable of using all aspects of our experience to power us, capable of changing course when needed, capable of staying the course too.

When you realize that you are a learner, creating and sharing your stories about life, and that you are entitled, because you are human, to contribute, then you become more powerful. You can put down and pick up stories with ease and the ones that harm you become simply laughable. You either don't pick up the stories designed to confine you, or you use them to become stronger, to learn and help others. You can care about others' views without allowing those views to change you without your permission. You can carry complexity, hold ambiguity, and know that you will not crumble if you need to wait in not-knowing for a while. You become a powerful social creator that no government and no corporation and no family member can easily control.

That's my aim in storytelling. Give people a new story, and they'll be at peace until things change and the story no longer works. Teach people to make a new story when needed, and they can make and share peace forever.

AFTERWORD

Exploring the Health Science in
Fat, Pretty, and Soon to Be Old

by Linda Bacon, PhD

Kimberly Dark is my hero. She writes from the heart, with poignancy and rawness that gets inside me. From my decades of challenging the pervasive "fat is bad" rhetoric, I know that anytime someone asserts that the problem for fat people isn't their bodies but abuse from society, bigotry kicks back. Particularly when it comes from someone with the audacity to be "publicly fat" and unapologetic.

The kickback comes not just from the haters but also from those who profess to care, waging their War on Obesity under the auspices of concern for fat people's health. As if you can separate this war from a war against "obese" people.

It's all about health, the argument goes, not bias. Because obesity is supposedly linked to disease and early mortality, it's okay to vilify it. And vilify it we do, from medical exam rooms to boardrooms and dorm rooms. The conversation gets sidetracked, from one about representation to one about health. As if the dignity of a group should be contingent on whether its members are deemed healthy or eating "right."

I write this afterword first to remind readers not to get sidetracked. The expectation that we treat fat people with dignity and respect needs to be divorced from questions of whether a person is healthy or pursues health-enhancing behaviors. Concern about someone's well-being requires that we show tenderness, compassion, and love, not wage war.

That said, I understand how insidious the health admonitions are. Repeated again and again, by so-called experts and lay people alike, they get inside us, leaving most of us, fat and thin, with negative judgment about fat bodies.

I recently watched a fat acquaintance defend herself after her mom's heartfelt, "Sweetie, I'm worried for you. I want to see you live a long, healthy life." This was prelude to her suggesting a diet. My friend's response: "But mom, I *am* healthy. Blood pressure and cholesterol levels, all good. I cook from the farmer's market and go to my spinning class regularly."

Her health status isn't unusual. Many fat people live without the complications of diabetes or heart disease. In fact, the majority do, though you'd never know it from the dire warnings. Many too eat well and exercise regularly. The research even shows that fat people don't eat more calories than thinner people, again a fact many consider unbelievable given the power of stereotype. There's a world of difference between what the data shows and popular assumptions.

I get my friend's defensiveness. She's tired, like most fat people, of being automatically read as sick. So she jumps to defensive posturing, claiming her space as the exception, the "good fatty." Her defensive assertion isn't wrong, but it distracts from the real issue. And sells out those who are sick or not dedicated to "self-improvement."

Mom is concerned. But where's her righteous anger at the airline that charges her daughter for two seats, making business travel cost-prohibitive and weakening her opportunity for job advancement? It's the daily crap like that that plays into her daughter's risk for diabetes, much more so than whether she eats her veggies. Let's name it for what it is: mom's concern is really one of many, many microaggressions, daily and unrelenting, that constitute her daughter's most insidious health risk.

The next time someone expresses concern about health, reframe it: fat bodies are not the problem; the real problem is the positing of certain bodies as the problem.

Just about everything we think we know about health and weight is wrong. Let me briefly walk you through the weight and health minefield. Right now, that minefield is littered with two treacherous assumptions. One is that fat kills. The second is that being fat will make you sick.

Does fat kill? Let's look at the facts.

To write my dissertation, I had to review the evidence that obesity increases mortality. And guess what? I couldn't find it.

In fact, there are about forty peer-reviewed epidemiologic studies on this topic, and all but a handful contradict the popular wisdom that fat kills. What most studies show is that people considered overweight and mildly or moderately obese live at least as long as or longer than people deemed normal weight. The data are a little more complicated at the extremes of underweight or obesity, so I won't get into that here, even though the practical application (treating people with respect!) works at the extremes too. But understand that I am talking about the vast majority of so-called overweight and obese people in this discussion.

Some of the most comprehensive data on weight and mortality comes from government statisticians at the Centers for Disease Control, using data from the highly respected National Health and Nutrition Examination Study (NHANES), the largest nationally representative cohort of U.S. adults. Their results, published in the Journal of the American Medical Association (JAMA), found that people in the overweight category lived longest, and people who were mildly or moderately obese, lived as long as those in the normal weight category. They also acknowledge that "[this] finding is consistent with other results reported in the literature."

Okay, so we don't have evidence that fat is the killer it's made out to be, you may be thinking, but it clearly causes disease.

Does it? Well, let's see.

If yellow teeth are common among people with lung cancer, do yellow teeth cause cancer? If bald men are prone to heart disease, does losing your hair make your ticker go bad? Of course not. Epidemiology shows us relationships but not causality. It shows an association between baldness and cardiovascular problems, for instance, but not the fact that elevated testosterone is implicated in both. And common sense tells us that yellow teeth, like lung cancer, can result from smoking.

Likewise, there are many factors that confuse the relationship between weight and health.

For example, consider fitness. The Cooper Institute in Dallas, Texas, has been gathering data on a large group of patients, examining the question of what's more important, fitness or fatness. Their research has been providing a consistent answer to the question for two decades now: when fitness is considered, body mass index (BMI) is almost irrelevant. In fact, fat but fit people fare much better than "normal" weight people who are unfit.

Next, consider discrimination and stigmatization. It is tough to live in a fat body in the United States (and most "developed" countries), socially and otherwise. Those of you who are not fat, think about what it must be like for larger people—that is, most of us—to confront daily in the papers, magazines, television shows, and commercials messages that their bodies are unattractive and constitute a horrifying public health crisis. To hear assumptions from dietitians and other health-care practitioners that because of a physical characteristic, their weight, they must be unhealthy and engaging in poor self-care. Everyone, fat or thin, is severely harmed by this message. It teaches all of us to see larger people as problematic and to fear becoming fat ourselves.

There are few legal protections, despite well-established facts that heavier people are less likely to be hired, promoted, or make comparable money to thinner people working in the same positions, and that they receive less adequate medical care. Weight bullying has steadily increased over the years and is now the most commonly reported form of bullying.

The resultant stress can initiate or aggravate some so-called "obesity-related" conditions, like diabetes and hypertension, helping to explain why they're often associated with weight.

For those who try to reduce, whether freelance or under doctor's orders, only a tiny minority keep weight off more than a couple years.

Most regain the weight regardless of whether they maintain their diets or exercise programs. It is well established that biological safeguards—some we understand and others we don't—cause our bodies to resist long-term weight loss. Failure to maintain weight loss is not a personal failure of will.

As for "try, try again," that's even worse: weight-cycling (also known as yo-yo dieting, where dieters go through cycles of weight loss followed by regain) has been found to cause some of the very conditions, like cardiovascular disease, weight losers seek to avoid. (Fat but stable-weight people log better health outcomes.) Evidence is scarce, in any case, that losing weight prolongs life. The vast majority of studies show that weight losers have decreased longevity, even when the loss is intentional.

Don't misunderstand, I'm not suggesting that everyone who is fat is healthy. I am not suggesting that everyone is at an ideal weight. I am not dismissing the notion that weight affects health. Nor am I suggesting that behavior doesn't matter.

What I am saying is that the relationship between weight and health has been wildly exaggerated. And that by focusing on fat and weight rather than body respect, we both do damage and miss our opportunity to make changes that *have* proven to be successful.

This war on obesity has caused far more health damage than can ever be attributed to high weight. By stigmatizing fat and fat people, it is creating stress (a known contributor to many of the diseases we blame on "obesity") and supporting discrimination. By inducing us to invest in useless efforts at weight control, it has resulted in rampant preoccupation with food and weight, disordered eating habits, and billions in wasted dollars. And, by focusing the medical community on fat over other factors, it is causing us to overlook more pernicious—and more effectively addressable—sources of disease. Missed diagnoses and reduced quality care are well documented, as is reluctance to seek medical care to avoid the negative judgment and stigmatization.

When health is our concern, we stand on much firmer ground by focusing on improving health directly, rather than using weight as a mediator. When we turn our focus to what *really* matters in promoting health.

Don't get fooled by the public health campaigns to get us moving or eating our fruits and veggies. Sure, diet and exercise are two of many factors that matter, but even combined they are not the main determinants of health. In fact, all told, health behaviors account for less than a quarter of differences in health outcomes between groups, according to the Centers for Disease Control and many well-established experts.

Social differences actually account for most of society's stark health differences. Suffering oppression, discrimination, or marginalization—and the stress of poverty—leads to worse health outcomes than those experienced by people afforded greater privilege.

The real crisis lies in the toxic stigma placed on certain bodies and the impact of living with inequity—not the numbers on a scale. The more we stigmatize fatness and glorify thinness, the less we tackle the real problems at the heart of health: classism, racism, sexism, a corporate structure that profits from our ceaseless dieting, and a reluctance to embrace body diversity, accepting and appreciating human bodies in all our wonderful and amazingly different forms, including size, shape, color, gender, age, and physical ability.

Let's all do our part in creating change. As Kimberly often says, "We are creating the world, even as it creates us."

REFERENCES

Du Bois, W. E. B. 1903. *The Souls of Black Folk*. New York: Dover Publications.

Essig, Laurie. 2010. *American Plastic: Boob Jobs, Credit Cards, and the Quest for Perfection*. New York: Beacon Press.

Goffman, Erving. 1956. *The Presentation of Self in Everyday Life*. Edinburgh: University of Edinburgh, Social Sciences Research Center.

hooks, bell. 2013. *Writing beyond Race: Living Theory and Practice*. New York: Routledge.

Mull, Amanda. "Body Positivity Is a Scam." *Vox*, June 5, 2018, https://www.vox.com/2018/6/5/17236212/body-positivity-scam-dove-campaign-ads.

Schonfielder, Lisa, and Barb Wiesner. 1983. *Shadow on a Tightrope: Writings by Women on Fat Oppression*. San Francisco: Aunt Lute Books.

Solnit, Rebecca. 2013. *The Faraway Nearby*. New York: Penguin Group.

Steele, Claude M. 2010. *Whistling Vivaldi: How Stereotypes Affect Us and What We Can Do*. New York: W. W. Norton.

Wann, Marilyn. 1998. *Fat!So? Because You Don't Have to Apologize for Your Size*. Berkeley: Ten Speed Press.

From the afterword:
Flegal, Katherine M., et al. "Excess Deaths Associated with Underweight, Overweight, and Obesity." *Journal of the American Medical Association* 293, no. 15 (2005): 1866.

ACKNOWLEDGMENTS

I'm so pleased that this book found a home with AK Press. It's been wonderful working with Charles, Zach, and Suzanne. I appreciate their skill and dedication to the values the press upholds. I'm honored to be in their company and the company of other AK Press authors.

Thanks are due to all those who read or heard my essays and stories about social life over the twenty-plus years that I've been publishing and performing. They've taught me how to write, what's important, and how to compassionately reveal the things that I may see a bit earlier and a bit more vividly than some.

Thank you to Dr. Lynda Dickson, who was the first to teach me to see the social world vividly, via a sociological lens, and to introduce me to writers whose work was not only rigorous but accessible. We met in 1987. She was the first black-woman-scholar I learned from in person and her persistent ability to be all three of those things in every interaction was an invaluable model for my own life. Our discussions over the years, though they've become less frequent, informed how I think about intersecting oppressions as both analogous and different. She has also influenced how I argue—hopefully—with humility, love, and a lot of curiosity intact.

Thank you to all of those who read and offered comments on early versions of this manuscript, fully and in pieces. Carol McGrath, Rebecca Rubenstein, Linda Bacon, and others. I appreciated being challenged by astute rejections though I also believe it's taken way too long for this book to come to print. As a culture, we are so recently speaking openly about the intersections of body identities and how appearance influences our lives. I've been speaking and writing about these things for years, doing my part, but wow, there is much to do and I'm so grateful that younger writers are already finding traction for their work on these themes. Go, darlings, go, go!

For my part, I'll continue to hone my skill and effectiveness at writing and creativity. In some ways they are separate pursuits, wedded in service of expressing an actionable vision. I hope all people become liberated in ways we can't even yet name. I pledge myself to do better and offer gratitude for all who help me see my way, though growth can be challenging. May we come to see discomfort and apprehension as part of the package marked freedom.

I accept that my work fails and I will keep doing my part. As an example, my writer-thinker-friend, Sonya Renee Taylor, pointed out that the phrasing of a certain point in the introduction to this book caused her pain. Could I not find another way to accomplish the same meaning, without re-traumatizing the black women who read that line? I'm sorry to say, I could not. I'm not that good yet. I'm committed to creatively discussing painful topics while inspiring hope and illuminating ability. With practice, I hope to do it more consistently. I am so grateful for the honesty and discussion she offered to prompt my effort.

Lastly, writers need time, space, and community in which to write. Some of this book was written at the Djerassi Writing Retreat, some at Dickinson House and some at CSU Summer Arts. The rest was written in my living room, where I thank the ancestors, the sea, land, and sky for the life I have every day.

To read my books and essays or attend my performances and retreats, visit kimberlydark.com.

AK Press is small, in terms of staff and resources, but we also manage to be one of the world's most productive anarchist publishing houses. We publish close to twenty books every year, and distribute thousands of other titles published by like-minded independent presses and projects from around the globe. We're entirely worker-run and democratically managed. We operate without a corporate structure—no boss, no managers, no bullshit.

The FRIENDS OF AK program is a way you can directly contribute to the continued existence of AK PRESS, and ensure that we're able to keep publishing books like this one! FRIENDS pay $25 a month directly into our publishing account ($30 for Canada, $35 for international), and receive a copy of every book AK PRESS publishes for the duration of their membership! Friends also receive a discount on anything they order from our website or buy at a table: 50% on AK titles, and 20% on everything else. We have a FRIENDS OF AK ebook program as well: $15 a month gets you an electronic copy of every book we publish for the duration of your membership. You can even sponsor a very discounted membership for someone in prison.

Email friendsofak@akpress.org for more info, or visit the FRIENDS OF AK PRESS website: https://www.akpress.org/friends.html.

There are always great book projects in the works—so sign up now to become a FRIEND OF AK PRESS, and let the presses roll!